More praise for *The Journey Through Heartache* from community leaders, pastors, and professionals.

"Dr. Greg Neal has 'hit the nail on the head' with his analysis on grief and the journey we must take as we move from loss to recovery."
— Commander William L. Cochran,
United States Navy, Retired

"The loss of a loved one, especially a child, shakes our very foundation. Dr. Neal's book helps to guide us to solid ground in a loving and practical way."
— Rhonda Woolwine, M.D.

"Greg Neal is a man who has been to the school of suffering and has returned with wisdom beyond his years. This book is a must for all who have experienced loss in their lives."
— Pastor Bill McSpadden, D.D.

"This book was written not from reference books in a brightly lit office, but from the bedside of a dying child — not with ink, but with tears of hurt and love. Thank you for your willingness to take us along on a journey that no one wants to make, but can change our lives like nothing else."
— Pastor Mike Holloway, D.D.

"The compassion, courage, and strength found in this book is truly inspirational."
— Carrie Moon, R.N.

"We never know when a heartache will come, and we are usually not prepared to know how to react. *The Journey Through Heartache* can help us deal with our grief."
— Mark Richt, Head Football Coach,
University of Georgia

"Read Greg Neal's book on the answers for loss of life. You may need it one day."
— Bobby Bowden, Head Football Coach,
Florida State University

"As a retired veteran of the Vietnam War, I can relate to grief. As I served my country, I saw countless comrades fall in battle, and I came to understand that everyone has his own way of dealing with grief. I believe we can all learn from the experience of Greg Neal and the strength that he has displayed during the most difficult of times."
— Donald J. Chitty,
Vietnam Veteran

The Journey Through Heartache

The Journey Through Heartache

A Guide to Understanding and Dealing with Grief

Dr. Greg Neal

Published in Orange Park, Florida, by Berean Publications.

Library of Congress Cataloging-in-Publication Data

Neal, Gregory M.
The journey through heartache: a guide to understanding and dealing with grief / Greg Neal
p. cm.

ISBN 0-9771829-0-8

Library of Congress Control Number: 2005931985

Printed and bound in the United States of America.

This book is dedicated to my wonderful daughters:

To Alyssa,
My oldest daughter, you made many sacrifices so your sister, Amanda could be cared for. You were such a source of strength during this trying time.

To Anna,
My youngest daughter, you have brought joy back into my life.

I love you both.
When you truly begin to understand the loss of your sister, I hope this book will be a help to you.

In Memory Of
Amanda Christine Neal
11/30/00 - 8/14/01

Table of Contents

Section Three – Recovery

Foreword
Testimonial of Coach Bobby Bowden

My wife and I have been married for fifty-six years. We have six children along with our children's six spouses, and twenty-one grandchildren. With this many people in our immediate family, one might wonder how long this number will stay the same without tragedy. In September 2004, we found out. On Labor Day, my son-in-law and grandson left our family outing at 4:00 p.m. to return home (120 miles away) so my grandson could attend high school football practice. About two hours later the Florida Highway Patrol knocked on my door to tell me John Madden, my son-in-law, and Bowden Madden, my grandson, had been killed immediately in an auto accident. We stood there in shock!

What would you do if you've never had this happen to you? We all expect our parents to die before us, but the younger ones??? Read this book on the answers for the loss of life; you may need it one day.

Bobby Bowden

Preface

A local newspaper interviewed me about my book, *An Angel Among Us*, and all of the things that I had experienced when my daughter, Amanda, died. The reporter that did the interview was amazed by how well he felt I had handled this terrible ordeal. I explained as best I could that I had determined not to let this tragedy beat me.

After my daughter's death, I was amazed at the amount of people who called upon me for counseling to help them with a loss. The worst event in my life had opened a door for me to help many people. Hardly a week goes by that someone does not contact me about a family member or a friend who is going through a loss. Many times I have knocked on a door of a stranger or entered the hospital room of someone I have never met and offered my help in any way possible.

I can not tell you how wonderful it feels to use my own experiences to help other people. It is my sincere desire to use my heartache to help others through their own heartache. It is my passion to help all those that I can to not only survive their loss but also regain the joy in life that they never thought they would experience again.

Please allow me to share my experiences and the experiences of others to help you through your heartache. I did my best to write this book not as a lecturer from behind a podium, but as someone who is traveling the same journey that you are traveling and living with a hurt just as you are.

Introduction: Directions for the Journey Through Heartache

There are several times a year when it is necessary for me to travel. The most enjoyable trips are the ones I choose to take. However, from time to time there are trips that are necessary for me to take that I would rather not take. Whatever the occasion of my travel, I believe the shorter the trip the better.

There have been occasions for me to travel across country. I live in Florida, but my wife grew up in California; consequently, we have taken several trips from Florida to California. There are several means of travel to make this trip. We could travel by car or travel by train, but we have always chosen the quickest means of travel which is to fly. All of these means of travel would get us to our destination. However, we chose the quickest means of travel.

If we had chosen to drive, we could have seen some wonderful sights along the way. We could stop to see a ball game or enjoy an amusement park. We could visit family along the way or stop in a big city. We could see the Mississippi River or witness the grandeur of the Grand Canyon. If time were not a factor, we could visit every other state in the continental United States before finally arriving in California.

We may choose a different means of travel than someone else. It might take us more or less time than someone else to reach our destination. Whether traveling by plane, train, or automobile, the important thing is that we all reach our destination.

It is important for you, the reader, to realize that heartache and tragedy set us on a journey. That journey is from loss, through grief, and to recovery. Look at the map of the United States. For the sake of illustration, we will say the state of Florida is loss. Having experienced a loss in our lives sets us on a journey seeking recovery. For the sake of illustration, we will say that California is recovery. There are many states that separate Florida and California. There are mountain ranges and bodies of water that present obstacles to  the traveler. There are heavily populated areas as well as sparsely populated areas. Likewise there is distance between loss and recovery. We will let all of the states in between Florida and California represent grief. It is an unavoidable fact that you must travel through grief to get to recovery.

This book will show you how to make the journey from loss to recovery by traveling through grief. You must complete this journey. At times it will be very hard, but keep your destination in mind. Use this book as your guide along the journey, and may it be a help along the way.

SOME THINGS TO CONSIDER ALONG YOUR JOURNEY

1. You must decide to begin your journey.
2. You must understand it can be a long journey.
3. Along the way there are mountains and valleys. (Ups and downs)
4. Along the way there are large cities and unpopulated deserts. (Periods of companionship and loneliness)
5. The journey is quicker and easier if you allow others to travel with you.
6. How fast you take the journey is up to you.
7. Faster is not always better. (Make any necessary stops along the way.)
8. In spite of how difficult the journey becomes, remember each day is one day closer to your destination.

Consider this book a road map. Make notes in it, highlight it, read, and reread the instructions that make your journey easier.

1

You Must Take Action

Every so often you hear someone make a statement or you read something in a book that changes you. It is perhaps a quote or a principle that inspires you. This eventually becomes a driving force in your life. I had an experience like this a few months before my daughter, Amanda, died. I was having a conversation with a man by the name of Barry Fuller. Barry is an attorney and has been a good friend for many years. In the course of our conversation, he made a statement. When I heard it, the words bounced around my head for a moment before finally settling in my heart. **"People who make a difference take action."** These words may not have been significant to Barry, but from that day forward those words have compelled me to accomplish many things.

Allow me to use myself as an example. I watched my daughter suffer for eight months. After twelve days on a ventilator, she was forced to endure spinal taps, daily shots, high fevers, and seizures. Only someone who has watched his child deal with physical pain and suffering understands the horror that I am talking about. Holding her in my arms and listening to her whimper in pain and discomfort is not something I will soon forget. After months of daily struggle, Amanda passed away. Even though the doctors had told us she would likely not live past the age of two, I was not prepared for my daughter to be taken from me. I knew this would cause much pain, but I could not have anticipated the magnitude of the hurt I felt. It was also extremely difficult to see my wife hurt as well. I knew that there was nothing that I could say or do to ease her pain. Perhaps the most difficult thing I have ever had to do was explain to my oldest daughter that Amanda would not be coming home again. I will never forget the puzzled look on her face when she came home the day Amanda died. She ran into our living room where Amanda normally was only to find the portable crib where Amanda normally lay put away. She asked why Amanda had not come home from the hospital. I tried to explain to her that Amanda was with Jesus now. Of course, being only three years old at the time, Alyssa did not understand; and she told me that she wanted her sister to stay with her.

We were obviously devastated over the loss of Amanda. The funeral was especially hard. The void that is left by the loss of a loved one is not easy to get used to. So many things such as sounds, smiles, and pictures reminded us of what we had been through.

I am not writing of this experience so that you might have sympathy for me. I am sharing some of my experiences with you in this book to send a message of hope. During this low point of

> *I am sharing some of my experiences with you in this book to send a message of hope.*

my life, these words rang in my ears—*Take Action*. I determined that my heartache would not defeat me. I would not recover from this on my own. Time would not heal these wounds. My life could essentially be over, or I could decide to do something about my circumstances. From that point, God has allowed me to do several things. First, I determined to recover. The sorrow is still very real, but I have learned to try to control it instead of the sorrow controlling me. I started a foundation that helps families who have a sick child or who unfortunately have a child pass away. This foundation has made a great impact on many lives. This is the second book that I have written and had published, and I have plans for several more. I do grief counseling on a regular basis. It is rewarding to make a difference by helping others deal with their grief. I have also taught much of the contents of this book in grief seminars.

I have not listed these accomplishments to magnify what I have done or myself. Many of the reasons I have been able to do these things are found in this book. I have shared these things as proof of the statement that my friend made to me on that fateful day. People who take action truly can make a difference. That difference is in their own life as well as the lives of others.

I hope you will realize that you too must take action to make a difference. Allow me to give you three very easy steps to take in order to make a difference in your own life, the lives of your loved ones, and even in the lives of strangers.

I.   FINISH THE BOOK.

You must complete this book. If you are battling grief, there are days that you will not feel like reading. Read very little or pick up the book the next day. This book will take you from your loss and carry you to a place you want to be—recovery. If you are to make a difference, you must determine to complete this book. The information you will find will empower you to overcome life's cruelties. This book will help you.

II.   APPLY WHAT YOU LEARN.

The information in this book comes from my own personal experiences as well as countless hours of research and interviews with other people. The information in this book is greatly beneficial to you but only if you apply it. The easiest way to apply the information is to incorporate it into your life on a daily basis. The "Grief Tips" are especially helpful for this. You will find "Grief Tips" throughout the book. These are practical bits of advice that will help you incorporate the contents of this book into your life. Do not just read the book; apply the book.

III.   PASS ON WHAT YOU LEARN TO SOMEONE
       ELSE.

If you are reading this book because of your own grief, then there is probably someone else very close to you who is grieving also. In my case, my wife also lost a child. My parents lost a grandchild. My brothers lost a niece. Determine who else you know that could benefit from this information. Remember you must take action to make a difference. Someone else could be depending on your help to recover.

Tell others who are grieving the information you learn from this book. Perhaps a phone call telling them "what you discovered about loss" will be just what they need. If the book is helpful to you, pass it on to someone else to read, or you could buy them a copy. Tell them about the website *www.lossgriefandrecovery.com.* This is a great source of grief help. Determine to find some way to pass on what you learn.

People who make a difference take action. Remember that statement. I have, and it has made a great difference in my life. It does not matter what your loss is or why you are grieving; just determine not to let it defeat you. Take action today!

SECTION ONE — LOSS

2

Grief Defined

What is grief? This seems like a simple enough question. The answers will vary depending on who you ask. Webster's Dictionary summarizes grief as the sorrow felt after the loss of a loved one. I looked up the word *grief* in several dictionaries, and they all gave similar answers. However, to the reader who is grieving, this one-sentence definition hardly sums up the vast plethora of emotions that you are feeling. I have counseled with many people who did not even realize all the feelings they were experiencing, so they could not have given an adequate answer. Without question, there are some who are grieving who do not even realize that what they are feeling is grief.

WHAT CAUSES GRIEF?

Grief is the natural, emotional reaction to loss in our lives. Grief is the body's response when we experience great loss. Loss comes in many different forms. Obviously, the greatest sense of loss is the death of a loved one. Let us look at different forms of loss that can trigger grief.

- Death of a loved one
- A loved one with an ongoing or terminal illness
- A change in one's own health
- Lost dreams
- Miscarriage
- The end of a relationship (divorce, son or daughter leaving home, etc.)
- A traumatic event in one's life
- Loss of financial security
- The loss of a job
- Passed over for a promotion
- Job relocation

Loss is not just the death of a loved one. Any of these losses mentioned can cause us to grieve. It is very important to understand that during a crisis or tragedy, most people will experience a combination of losses. An example of this is when you find out a loved one has a terminal illness, and after some time, the loved one dies. You grieve while the person is still alive and after he has passed away. This was the case with my wife and me. Although we did not realize it at the time, we began grieving when we were told that Amanda would not live very long.

The following is an excerpt from Chapter 11 in the book, *An Angel Among Us.*

I was devastated. My wife, mother-in-law, and I walked to the elevator. After each step I took, I did not think that I could take another. While we were in the elevator, I took a deep breath as my knees buckled. As we left the elevator and exited the building, our lives would never be the same.

We had just heard the worst news of our lives. We had a follow-up appointment with the neurologist. Even after learning that Amanda was having seizures and her EEG was abnormal, I still did not expect to hear what the doctor had told us. I believed that the doctor would have some solution for us. Naively, I thought every thing would turn out fine. The news we received was like a punch in the face. It did not take us long to see that the optimism we had entered the doctor's office with would not be leaving with us.

It was as if someone was sucking the air right out of the room. The neurologist, Dr. Harry Abram, was solemn and matter of fact. I guess this was the hardest part of his job. My wife and I had a seat in one of the side rooms while my mother-in-law waited in the waiting room. When Dr. Abram entered the room, he wasted little time giving us the news. He began by reviewing with us the difficulties that Amanda had faced so far. He then gave us his diagnosis of Amanda's condition.

The doctor began by telling us that Amanda had a form of epilepsy. Something in Amanda's brain was not working right. He did not know exactly what was wrong, and he did not think that we ever would. He told us that Amanda had early infantile myoclonic encephalopathy and perhaps Ohtohara's Syndrome. Obviously, I did not exactly know what this meant. He explained that this was the name of the type of epilepsy that Amanda showed the most characteristics of. He also pointed out that he did not have all of the answers concerning her condition.

The question that burned in my mind at this time was simple. "What does this mean?" As if the doctor could read my mind, he proceeded to tell us what we could expect in Amanda's future. She obviously would not develop at a normal pace. He told us that it was rare that a baby in Amanda's condition lived past infancy. In his opinion, he did not think that Amanda would live past her second birthday. If she did live that long, he thought she would be an invalid. As you can imagine, the longer that we were in that room, the harder it was to control our emotions. By now my wife was crying, and tears were beginning to run down my cheeks. My wife excused herself so she could go tell her mother the bad news leaving me alone with the doctor.

While my wife was out of the room, I asked the doctor to go over everything with me again. It sounded just as bad the second time. I asked him how we could expect her to die. He said that usually these babies died of pneumonia or blood infection. At this time, my wife came back into the room.

The doctor then proceeded to give us our options to treat Amanda's condition. He told us that there were treatments that he wanted to try that could help Amanda's seizures. At this time he wanted to start her on a drug called Klonopin. We were to be cautious because of its side effects which were over sedation and drooling. He again apologized for not having any good news for us. As we prepared to leave, the one thing that was prevalent in my mind was that instead of the hurts and heartaches coming to an end, they were just beginning.

The drive home from the doctor's office was awkward. I did not know what to say to my wife at this point. I was trying to be a comfort to her while I was trying to sort things out in my own mind. The only assurances I could offer her at this point were that God knew and that everything was going to be all right. At this point I was saying these things to calm my fears as much as I was trying to be a source of strength for my wife. During the thirty minutes that it takes to travel home, we discussed when and how we would tell our families.

We decided that we would stop by the church to tell my father what we had been told by the doctor. He knew, as well as the rest of the family, that we had an appointment earlier that day. We figured someone would call soon to find out what we had been told. Heather's mother dropped us off, and she took Amanda home. My father was standing in the foyer when we arrived, and I asked if we could talk to him for a second. He saw our expressions and could tell that what we needed to tell him was serious. We walked back to his office where my wife and I sat on his couch. We told him what the doctor had told us. He was quiet for a few seconds as he began to cry. He quickly gathered his composure, and he began to offer some words of encouragement. He called my mother who was shopping and told her that she needed to come to his office because we needed her there. He left his office while we waited on my mother to arrive. I did not know it at the time; but while my father was gone, he told two of my brothers, Brent and Mark, the bad news. After a few minutes, my father came back into his office along with my mother. He began to tell her what we had told him a few minutes earlier. At this point, I had not cried since we had left the hospital. When I saw my mother begin to cry, I could not keep my composure any *longer. After exchanging hugs and assurances that God was in control, we left the church and went home.*

When we first arrived home, we did very well dealing with everything that we had been told that day. Later that evening my parents came over to see Amanda. They stayed for a little while, and we enjoyed their company. After they left for home, the reality of the bad news that we had been given began to sink in. That evening we shed a lot of tears. I spent time alone asking God for strength and wisdom to get through this. My wife and I spent time together crying and asking God for a miracle.

When March 9, 2001, ended, we were hurt, confused, and scared. After what we had already faced, we did not believe that we could endure much more. Needless to say, we were very uncertain about the future. We were clinging to the hope that everything would be all right. As I lay in bed, I thought of the possibility of miracles and hopes of Amanda getting better. When this day ended, it ended as so many had over the last several months. It ended with the parents of a sick child, whom they loved, crying themselves to sleep.

When I penned the account of that horrible day six months after I had experienced it, I still did not realize the feelings that I was experiencing were grief. As soon as I realized my daughter's future was grim, I experienced an incredible loss. My emotional reactions were grief.

Another form of loss that my wife and I experienced was the ongoing care of our sick child. Each day that we cared for her, we were reminded that her condition would not get better and that she would never be normal. As I look back on those days now, I understand that not only did we have to deal with the tiring responsibility of caring for our child, but we were also grieving and did not even realize it.

The following is an excerpt from Chapter 18 in the book *An Angel Among Us.*

At this point in Amanda's life, my wife and I felt as if there were nothing else we could do for her. We knew that there was not much hope that Amanda would live a normal life. The important thing to us now was to love and care for her as much as possible.

Fortunately, by now we were well equipped to care for her. We had acquired much of the same equipment that was used in the hospital. We turned our living room into a temporary hospital room. This room was equipped with oxygen, an ambu bag, a suction machine, and a monitor. Even though we never felt very comfortable using this equipment, we were glad we had it.

We were somewhat overwhelmed at all that we had to do to care for Amanda. Heather was incredible at caring for her. Amanda was fed on a strict schedule, and she had many medicines that she had to take as well. Amanda required twenty-four-hour-a-day care. We had to keep a constant watch on her in case she began choking. Because of this, we never could relax in our own house. We were always tense, waiting for something bad to happen. She had choking episodes often. Usually she would spit up or choke on her saliva. She would then stop breathing which would set off her alarms on her monitor. We would have to use the suction machine to clear her throat, and then use the ambu bag to give her oxygen. This became a daily routine.

It was very tiring. We rotated shifts trying to stay as rested as possible. However, I still had to be at work; so Heather had most of this responsibility. There was no one who could care for Amanda like Heather could. She took such good care of her. It was also a blessing having Heather's mom living with us. Since she was a nurse, she knew what to do when Amanda started choking. She also gave us relief when she was not working.

We kept this schedule for a couple of months. I knew that we could not keep it much longer. Then God performed a miracle for us. We were able to get some home nursing care to give us a break. This was supposed to be for a couple of weeks, but it was approved for a couple of months. This meant that eight hours a day a nurse would watch Amanda so we could rest. I was excited for several reasons. Heather could not continue the schedule that she was keeping. Even though no one could care for Amanda like she could, she had to have a break. This also meant that we could spend time with our oldest daughter, Alyssa. We had not been able to spend much time with her since Amanda was born.

Over this period of a few months, Amanda grew worse. She seemed to be having more seizures than before. The choking episodes became more and more frequent and seemed to become more and more severe. Whenever this happened, it was always so horrifying. As we watched the numbers on the monitor continue to drop, we knew that there was no doctor in the next room to call upon. We always knew that it was up to us to save her. This was such an overwhelming feeling, but it was gratifying when we were able to get her breathing again. I would tell my wife that not every parent knew what it was like to save the life of his child. We got to experience this almost every day.

Obviously, the greatest loss experienced was the death of our daughter. Even though we were grieving while we were caring for Amanda, we were still able to be with her and help her. When Amanda passed away, there was a great void; thus, we experienced the greatest form of loss.

The following is an except from Chapter 22 in the book *An Angel Among Us*.

The next morning Amanda was going to get to come home. We went to bed that night still apprehensive, but knowing that Amanda was in God's hands. As tired as we were, it was not uncommon for us to wake up every so often because of every thing on our minds.

At 6:45 a.m., we were awakened by the telephone. Even though we were planning to get up about this time, we were startled by the phone. I knew that it was someone from the hospital. My mother-in-law, who had stayed at the hospital overnight, was on the phone. She was crying so I could not understand what she was saying. I knew the situation was not good, but I could not believe how calm that I was. I told her to slow down because I could not understand her. She told me that we needed to get to the hospital fast. She said Amanda's heart rate began to drop during the night and was continuing to do so. I told my wife who was already getting ready what her mother had said. Amanda's heart had always been strong, so this was something new.

As we began to get ready to leave, my wife kept saying over and over that Amanda is going to Heaven. I told her that I also thought that she would be going to Heaven. Heather called my parents and told them that they needed to get to the hospital as fast as possible because Amanda was going to Heaven. After a few more minutes, we were ready to leave. We climbed into our van and prepared ourselves for the longest and most difficult ride of our lives.

Normally, at this time of the morning, it would take over an hour to get to the hospital. We did not know if we had this much time before Amanda went to Heaven. Even though Heather's mom did not say that this was the case, we both knew that she was not going to be with us much longer. Even though we were very sad, we had a peace and comfort about the situation.

As we drove to the hospital as fast as we could, our biggest concern was that we would not make it to the hospital fast enough. Fortunately, the traffic was not bad that morning. We arrived at the hospital around eight o'clock.

We took the elevator to the third floor. We rushed into the Intensive Care Unit. I will never forget the looks on the faces of the doctors and nurses as they watched us hurry to Amanda's room. Each face seemed to say, "I'm sorry." When we went into Amanda's room, Heather's mom and brother were there along with a hospital chaplain. When we got to Amanda's bedside, we could see that it would not be long before she went to Heaven. Heather rubbed

Amanda's head while I held her hand. By this time we could no longer hold back the tears. Through tears and sobs, Heather told Amanda that it was okay for her to go. Neither one of us wanted her to suffer any more. We had always told each other that we would know when it was time for Amanda to go. There was no doubt that this was her time.

After a few minutes, one of Amanda's nurses came in and told us that when Amanda's heart rate dropped she had to bag her with the ambu bag to bring her heart rate and oxygen level back up. We told her that we did not want this because it was time for her to go to Heaven. Some might wonder how we could do this, but it was not a difficult thing to do. We had watched her suffer so much, and we did not want this to be prolonged. We knew that God had decided that this was the time that He would take her to be with Him.

The nurse then asked if Heather wanted to hold her. Heather said she did, so the nurse turned off her monitors and put Amanda in Heather's lap. As I knelt beside Heather, we both told Amanda how much we loved her. We also told her that we would miss her, but that we were glad that very soon she would not suffer any more. Since the monitors were no longer on, we had no way of knowing whether or not Amanda was still alive. After a few more minutes the doctor came in and listened to her chest with the stethoscope. After a brief moment, the doctor nodded that she was gone. We burst into tears again, knowing that our daughter had died.

Less than a minute later, my parents came into the room. Heather was still holding Amanda, and I was still kneeling by her side. My dad walked up behind me and placed his hand on my shoulder. Without looking, I told him that Amanda was in Heaven. His response to me was that yes, she is. I took Amanda from Heather and placed her in her bed. Of course, everyone was weeping by this point. Everyone exchanged hugs and conveyed to each other how sorry they were. After a few more moments, everyone left so Heather and I could spend a few minutes alone with Amanda. We stood on either side of her bed, and once again loved on her a little bit more. After we felt that we were ready to go, I kissed Amanda on the forehead, told her that I loved her, and then we left the room.

When Amanda passed away, I was prepared to grieve. What I did not realize was that I had already been grieving for several months. I had faced difficult losses that had caused me to grieve. When I was first told that my daughter would pass away, I began to grieve. The daily care of my sick child had caused me to grieve. Of course, the death of my child caused me to grieve as well.

While I was preparing to write this book, I interviewed a lady by the name of Sharon Stanley. I have known Sharon most of my life. God has blessed her with a lot of talent in the area of music. She is a church pianist and is involved in music in many ways. As a pianist, she has her own recordings and is a talented teacher. She has also done the orchestration and production of several other tapes and CDs. She is an exceptional soloist and has traveled the country singing as a college student. She has now trained singing groups that have traveled the country. Gifted is a word that comes to mind when speaking of Sharon's musical abilities.

Why would someone possessing incredible talents and achieving great accomplishments be interviewed for a book on grief? Many years ago, Sharon was diagnosed with Rheumatoid Arthritis. This news was devastating. This disease has taken away many things that have been a large part of her life. She can no longer do all the things musically that she did before. Sharon told me that this disease has affected her two most basic but important responsibilities of being a wife and mother. Sharon initially was affected by her loss of health, but now feels the loss of ability to do all the things that she loves to do.

When I asked Sharon if she had grieved, she told me, "Yes." She realized that she was grieving because she had seen many of the warning signs of grief. I asked her if it would be accurate to say that she had been through the same grieving process as someone who had lost a loved one in death. She answered, "Yes and no." She said that she believed that she had been through the same grieving process, but did not think that she could comprehend the magnitude of the loss felt by someone who has lost a loved one. I want to bring out an important point from this statement. Sharon had gone through the same grieving process because we all grieve over loss. The magnitude of the loss or the grieving process may be different, but why we grieve is the same.

> *The magnitude of the loss or the grieving process may be different, but why we grieve is the same.*

In preparation for this book, I also interviewed a lady who had recently been divorced.

She explained that she had seen all of the signs and knew that the divorce was inevitable. With this loss obviously came many adjustments. She had to deal with the grief that this loss had brought into her life. She also realized that she had been grieving for some time before the divorce. There had been no relationship with her husband for some time. This fact had caused her to grieve this loss. She had been grieving the loss of a good relationship with her spouse before the divorce, and she was grieving the loss of having a spouse after the divorce.

What is grief? The best definition of grief is the sense of great loss. You do not have to decide to grieve. As soon as you experience the loss, you begin grieving even if you do not realize it. Everyone grieves. It is part of being human.

GRIEF TIP
Write down the loss that you have suffered that is causing you grief.

GRIEF TIP
After writing down the loss you have experienced, you probably have recognized the fact that you have been grieving longer than you first realized. Determine how long you have actually been grieving.

3

William and Shelly Grabow: An Example of Loss

I received a call on my cell phone the day after one of the several occasions the local news did a story on Amanda. On the phone was a lady who had seen my story on the news the previous night. She asked me if she could share her story with me. I was glad to listen, so I pulled my vehicle into a parking lot. For the next several minutes, I listened to a mother tell me through tears of her children. After she told her story, she asked if there was a way that I could help them. I was moved by what I had heard and promised to do all that I could.

It was several months before I actually made it to the home of the lady who placed the phone call that day. I am glad that I was finally able to meet Will and Shelly Grabow. I listened and watched them intently as they told me the needs that were a result of the story Shelly had shared with me that day on the phone. As they talked, I studied their faces. You could see the hurt in their eyes. You could almost feel the burden of sorrow that they seemed to carry on their shoulders.

I gave them some information and encouraged them the best that I could. I said good-bye and instructed them to call upon me at any time. I reassured them that I would help in any way that I possible could. As I left their home, I told myself that no one should have to experience the loss that they had experienced. I determined that others needed to hear their story.

Meet Will and Shelly Grabow, an example of loss.

Will and Shelly were excited to be expecting their first child. As I suppose all first-time parents do, they eagerly made a list of things to get done before the family's new addition arrived. However, these new parents did not have as much time as they thought to prepare for the newest member of the Grabow family. Five weeks before the baby's due date, Shelly was being prepared to deliver her first child. She was nervous but was filled with anticipation. Will was caught in this unexpected whirlwind. Although he was nervous too, he offered his support to Shelly.

Caleb Patrick Grabow was born on September 14, 2001. Because he was premature, it would be necessary for him to stay in the NICU (Neonatal Intensive Care Unit) for what was sure to be a short period of time. Although Will and Shelly were somewhat distraught over this fact, they were able to take comfort from the nurses' words of encouragement. "The healthiest baby in the NICU" is what they recall being told. At this point there was no reason to believe anything different. The only thing Caleb was having trouble doing was feeding. This is fairly common in premature babies, so this did not present a need to panic. Unfortunately, panic would soon become a feeling Will and Shelly was very familiar with.

Caleb stayed in the hospital after Shelly was

discharged. Will and Shelly made daily visits to spend time with their son. After each visit, they anticipated the day that Caleb would be strong enough to come home. On the twelfth day of Caleb's life, Shelly received a call from the hospital while she was at home. She was shocked at the news she received. The voice on the other end of the phone informed her that her son had become "floppy" in the nurse's arms while feeding. The message was conveyed loud and clear. Caleb was having trouble breathing.

Will and Shelly rushed to the hospital. Panic filled their hearts as they drove to the hospital. Within an hour of being reunited with Caleb, he stopped breathing. Once again panic took hold of Will and Shelly as the doctors and nurses scrambled to revive their son. Fortunately, these doctors and nurses were successful in their attempts to revive Caleb. He began breathing again, but this new development in his health was definitely a reason for concern.

Later that evening, Will and Shelly were informed of Caleb's need to be transferred to the local children's hospital. This transfer offered some comfort because the children's hospital would be better equipped to care for Caleb. However, Will and Shelly were informed that they would not be able to see Caleb until the next morning. As Caleb was loaded into the transport, Will and Shelly prayed that he would survive the trip. As the transport pulled away, panic reared its head once more. Would this be the last time that they ever saw their baby alive? As the taillights of the ambulance disappeared, Will and Shelly sat in the parking lot and began to weep.

The couple finally made it home to await the

anticipated morning. Around midnight the phone rang. As Shelly rushed to the phone, she wondered if this was the dreaded phone call that all parents fear. The neonatologist at the children's hospital informed her that Caleb was stable and receiving a blood transfusion. Shelly's racing heart began to slow as the news began to sink in. Shelly was then informed that they could see Caleb at ten the next morning.

There was no sleeping in the Grabow house that night. Worry and anticipation stood in the way of getting any rest. The next morning, Will and Shelly began the drive to the hospital. On the way, conversation was limited; but Shelly remembers telling Will that Caleb would be all right as long as his heart was okay. When they arrived at the NICU, the neonatologist took them to a private room to give them the worst news that a parent could receive. Will and Shelly were informed that Caleb had an inborn error of metabolism that affects the function of his heart. When Shelly heard the diagnosis, she recalled what she had told Will just a few minutes earlier in the car. At this point, she knew that her son was not going to make it. The doctor confirmed her fear by telling them that Caleb probably would not make it through the night.

Will and Shelly went to Caleb's room to spend as much time with him as possible. Shelly held Caleb in her arms and sang to him. Caleb opened his eyes one last time before taking his final breath. Shortly after midnight, Caleb died at just fourteen days old.

The following spring, Will and Shelly found out they were expecting another child. Because Caleb had a metabolic disorder, Will and Shelly decided to see a geneticist. When Shelly was fifteen weeks pregnant, she found out that the baby had a multi-cystic kidney and was diagnosed with Multi-cystic Dysplastic Kidney Disease. For the remainder of the pregnancy Will and Shelly would have to live with the fear that their second child would face the same fate as their first.

On December 31, 2002, Caden Nathaniel Grabow was born by emergency caesarean. When Caden was born, he had breathing difficulties. Finally, Will and Shelly were able to see Caden twenty-four hours later. He was breathing with a ventilator. It is a very traumatic thing for a parent to see his child hooked to a ventilator, but these parents were happy to have another child.

When Caden was three weeks old, Will and Shelly were told that he did not have the same disorder that Caleb had. This was great news. However, Caden's life has not been without struggle. When Caden was eight months old, his parents were told that Caden would need to have his left kidney removed. During the surgery panic began to become a familiar feeling once again. The fear of losing another child was an overwhelming prospect to deal with. After what seemed to be an eternity, the doctor emerged from the operating room to inform Will and Shelly of the surgery's success. Caden is doing well today and has had no signs of disease in his right kidney. Even though Caden had experienced some medical difficulties, Will and Shelly were excited to have another son.

Not much time had passed when Shelly found out she was expecting their third child. The uneasy feelings that were a result of losing their first child was balanced by the knowledge that Caden was okay. During a routine checkup, Shelly mentioned to her doctor that she had not felt the baby move in a while. The doctor placed Shelly on a fetal monitor. The monitor showed that the baby was having heart decelerations, which signified that the baby was in distress. Shelly was transferred to the hospital where she immediately had an emergency caesarean. Noah, the Grabow's third son, was born shortly thereafter. Noah was two pounds and fourteen ounces when he was born. Surprisingly, he was breathing on his own.

Three days later, the bad news was presented to the Grabows. Noah had the same disorder that his brother Caleb had died from. Because the doctors had some history available to them, they were able to start treatments on Noah. This seemed to be working well because Noah was bottle feeding and gaining weight. He was even healthy enough to take home a month later.

Two months had passed since Noah came home from the hospital. Will and Shelly enjoyed their growing family. The family had settled into a routine when without warning Noah suffered a metabolic crisis. When Will and Shelly arrived at the emergency room, Noah's breathing was very shallow. Once inside the hospital, Noah stopped breathing completely. Doctors struggled to revive Noah. Once again the familiar feeling of panic was present. Finally, the doctors were able to get Noah breathing again with the use of a respirator. This couple was once again faced with the prospect of losing another child.

The next forty days were days of struggle. Noah struggled with life while Will and Shelly struggled with watching their son suffer with the discomforts of his poor health. Noah fought many battles. He faced two more metabolic crises and several infections. Both of his lungs collapsed twice, and he battled fevers. He had to have a G-tube surgically placed so that he could be fed. Noah suffered a lot in those forty days. Will and Shelly suffered during those forty days also. Each day they were tortured with the realization that this could be the last day that they have with Noah. Finally, Noah suffered cardiomyopathy that led to heart failure. His struggle with life was over.

The Grabows are truly an example of loss. They have experienced twice what no parent should have to experience once. Since that day I first met them, their positive outlook in spite of their loss has impressed me. I hope their story has been a help in some way.

4

Secondary Loss

It was my third trip to New York City. This trip was much different than my previous two. This was the first time I had made the trip since September 11, 2001. I looked forward to visiting "Ground Zero", but I was dreading it as well. When I got off the subway and made my way from the subway tunnel, it took just a moment to see the impact of those horrible attacks. As I made my way toward the observation deck, many of the pictures and signs that I had seen on television were still hanging on a fence that lined the sidewalk. I walked up the wooden ramp to the observation deck. There were hundreds, if not thousands, of messages of support written along the walkway. I walked to the deck and looked into what was now a big hole where once the majestic Twin Towers stood. I thought about going to the top of one of the towers on my first visit to New York. The view was absolutely breathtaking. On my previous trips, this was definitely one of the highlights of my visit to New York. The buildings were so big; it just did not seem possible that they could be gone.

However, I knew they were gone. I recalled that day as I sat in front of the television watching the horrible event on the news. I still remember the footage of the planes crashing into the towers. I will never forget the sick feeling in my stomach as I watched the towers fall. As I stood on the observation deck, my eyes filled with tears just as they did while I was sitting in front of the TV. As an American, I had experienced loss. I did not know anyone who died that day. I did not have a relative who died in an act of heroism. However, I was an American, and all Americans had lost something that day.

Because of that day in September, our world has changed. We are facing challenges in everyday life that come from not only our primary loss, but also our secondary losses as well. One secondary loss is the loss of security. Every time I fly, I dread going through airport security. The fact that I now have to take off my shoes before I pass through the security checkpoint is not the loss of September 11. It is a direct result of September 11. The loss of security that the country must now deal with is the secondary loss. I am reminded of that day each time that I must deal with a result of that loss. We must deal with events in our everyday lives that are losses, but we do not recognize them as losses.

In Chapter 2, I have taken the time to express the idea that it is important for us to recognize our loss, to identify our loss, and to accept the fact that we have lost. We can not go around in a state of denial. When we face our loss, many times we do not realize all the losses that we have experienced. Likewise, we do not always identify all of our secondary losses.

What we need to do now is not just look at our loss, but look at what I call secondary losses. What losses have occurred because of our previous loss? Reflect on your current situation. What is it that you have lost? No doubt, some of you reading this book may have lost a loved one to death. Some of you may have experienced divorce. Some of you may have lost a job promotion. Perhaps you have lost your health. Whatever loss you have experienced, I want you to write it in the space provided. Think of all of the possible losses in your life. Perhaps referring to the list in Chapter 1 will help you identify your loss. My loss was a daughter. This is easy to identify as my primary loss. Whatever it is in your life, I urge you to identify it before you read any further.

Primary Loss _____

Amanda lost her health at a very early age. This was one of the primary losses that we had to deal with. Amanda was never able to do what healthy children could do. She did not feed as other babies. Amanda had to be fed through a tube. Amanda could not move from side to side or even lift her head. We had to help Amanda repeatedly with her breathing. Because my wife and I had a child who lost her health, we were forced to deal with secondary losses as well.

One of the secondary losses was a loss of rest. The schedule that had to be kept to care for Amanda meant periods of no sleep. When we did get to sleep for a few hours, we still would not feel rested. Another secondary loss was a loss of health. Because of the incredible strain, which included lack of rest, emotional stress and fatigue, and a change in eating habits, our health was affected. Eleven days after giving birth by caesarean section, my wife should have been resting on her way to recovery. Instead, she was sleeping in a chair used as a makeshift bed in the Intensive Care Unit. This did not help her physically. Even though several years have passed, I do not believe that my wife has recovered physically. In many ways, the secondary losses were what made the primary loss so devastating.

> *In many ways, the secondary losses were what made the primary loss so devastating.*

Another primary loss was that Amanda passed away. This was not the only loss that I experienced. The size of my family did not just go from four to three. There are a number of things that I lost as a result of losing Amanda. Let me explain.

My oldest daughter, Alyssa, and I spend a lot of time together. I lost that time that I would have had with Amanda when she passed away. I remember how excited my wife and I were when Alyssa took her first step. We never had that experience with Amanda. I remember when Alyssa lost her first tooth. This event was lost with Amanda when she passed away. When Alyssa turns sixteen, she will be old enough for me to take her to get her driver's license. I will never have that experience with Amanda. When the day comes for Alyssa to be married, I will have the privilege of walking Alyssa down the aisle. I do not have that to look forward to with Amanda. If time is one of the most valuable things that we can give someone, then lost time is a secondary loss.

My wife and I have a couple of photo albums filled

> *If time is one of the most valuable things that we can give someone, then lost time is a secondary loss.*

with pictures of Alyssa. We update these albums after every birthday and special event. If a stranger were to look through these albums, they would get a sense of all of the wonderful memories that my wife and I have been privileged to enjoy with Alyssa. If a stranger looked through the pictures of Amanda, they would notice right away that there are considerably fewer pictures of Amanda than there are of Alyssa. The difference in the number of pictures (or memories) can be summed up as secondary losses.

You have to deal with secondary losses. Many times there are losses that are going to carry on with you over long periods of time. Let us look at the typical divorcee. What do they lose? They do not just lose a husband or a wife. They have lost the celebration of anniversaries. They have lost the person who balanced the checkbook. The divorcee has lost the person who made sure the taxes were done. They have lost the one who raked the leaves and cut the grass. They have lost a confidant and a dinner companion. They have lost the one they went to church and social functions with.

Someone who loses a job has secondary losses. They did not just lose a job; they lost financial security. Along with losing some confidence, perhaps they lost their reputation as well.

Someone who was abused as a child must recognize all of his or her losses as well. They did not just lose their childhood. Along with a loss of innocence, they lose self-confidence, self-respect, dignity, and confidence in other people. These are all secondary losses.

Failing to identify all of the secondary losses is where a lot of people fail on their road to recovery. It is easy to identify the loss, but we do not take the time to identify the secondary losses. In order to put yourself in position to recover from your heartache, you have to identify all of your secondary losses.

When I think about the fact that I will never have certain memories with Amanda, all of the events surrounding her death are brought to mind again. My primary loss is now brought to the forefront of my mind because all of the secondary losses point to the primary loss. This forces me to deal with grief again. Each time I deal with a secondary loss, I have to decide the same thing that I had to decide with the primary loss. I have to decide how I am going to deal with it. There are people across the planet that experience loss, and they grieve the primary loss. However, they fail to understand that there are secondary losses that must be dealt with. Anyone who experiences loss must understand that to truly grieve your loss you must face and deal with the secondary losses as well.

> *My primary loss is now brought to the forefront of my mind because all of the secondary losses point to the primary loss.*

One of the ways that I have been able to help people who have experienced loss is by teaching a class on grief. One of those who attended my class was Charlotte Wright. Charlotte came because she had lost her husband to a heart attack many years ago. It did not take me long at all to realize that she dealt with the secondary losses of her husband's death on a daily basis. She explained to me that she not only lost a husband, but also lost her financial security, her best friend, a father for her youngest son, and eventually her home.

Each time she deals with a secondary loss, she is forced to deal with her primary loss all over again. Each time she struggles with finances, it reminds her that she lost her husband who was her financial security. The fact that she lost her home is a reminder that her husband is gone. Each time her son struggles with a particular situation, she is reminded that his father is no longer here. Every one of these things that she must deal with on a daily basis points her to the fact that her husband has passed away. Charlotte believes that she would not be able to deal with the loss of her husband if she chose to ignore the secondary losses that are a direct result of her husband's death.

Charlotte told me that she really had no idea before her husband's death that the secondary losses would be so hard to deal with. She described her secondary losses as "overwhelming". Why is she still overwhelmed after so many years? Isn't that enough time to move on to recovery? Not if she still must deal with secondary losses. The loss you have experienced might not have as many secondary losses. However, you must deal with them directly because they are directly linked to your primary loss.

I asked Charlotte what advice she would give to someone dealing with secondary losses. Her advice

> *To ignore your secondary losses is to ignore your primary loss.*

was simple yet right on target. "Don't ignore them." To ignore your secondary losses is to ignore your primary loss.

Perhaps, when you were a child your parents went through a divorce. You not only lost a normal family unit, but also lost many other things as well. A child whose parents divorce loses a mom or dad. Maybe they lose a counselor or a fishing buddy. They lose security or their childhood home. The child many times blames himself for the divorce causing him to lose self-esteem and confidence.

Someone who has a sickness or a disease must also deal with secondary losses. They can not do physically what they used to be able to do. Maybe their health keeps them from putting in the hours at something that they are used to doing. A job loss could result from a loss of health.

What is the "trickle down" effect of our loss? What are all the results of our loss? It is necessary for us to anticipate our secondary losses. If you have a loved one pass away, what are the other losses you will have to deal with? If you lose your health, you need to anticipate the changes in your life. When you have experienced loss, it is very difficult to look ahead because you must deal with the present situation. When we prepare ourselves for the secondary losses, we are helping ourselves deal with the primary loss.

Take a look at the chart on the next page. This chart summarizes everyone who has experienced loss.

The number of secondary losses is determined by the magnitude of the primary loss.

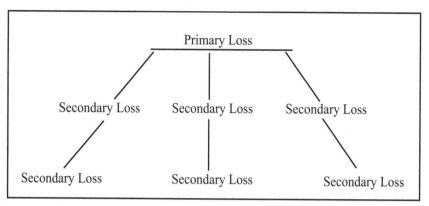

Earlier in the chapter, I had you write your primary loss. In the chart below, write your primary loss in the appropriate space. Underneath your primary loss, list all of the secondary losses that have occurred because of your primary loss. Include in this list the losses that you anticipate in the future. Take the time now to do this. It is important that you list everything possible.

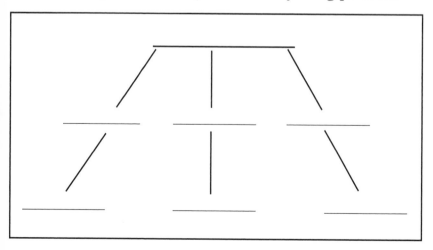

Now that you have filled in the chart, you have created a very powerful tool to use in your recovery process. Look at your list. You now have a checklist of losses that you must deal with. Perhaps it would be helpful to look over this list every day. Then you can mentally prepare to face the obstacles that come as a result of these losses.

5

How Loss Affects You Spiritually

Grief is a spiritual matter. I am amazed at the responses I sometimes get when making this statement. I have had people tell me that they do not believe in God, so He can not have anything to do with grief. "Grief can not be a spiritual matter because God does not want anyone to hurt." is a statement I have often heard. I believe I can explain why grief is a spiritual matter.

We know that grief is caused by a loss. When we experience loss, we begin to seek the reason behind it. When we are dealt heartache, we begin to ask questions. Why did this happen? Why did they leave me? Why did this happen to my loved one? What did I do to deserve this? Are we asking these questions of ourselves? If we knew the answers, we could have prevented the loss. The truth is that whether we realize it or not when we ask these questions, we are asking God. Whether we have a personal relationship with Him or not, we are seeking an answer from God. Loss in our life causes us to seek God.

There are three spiritual opportunities we have when we experience loss. Take advantage of any of these opportunities that you can.

1.   YOU HAVE THE OPPORTUNITY TO ACCEPT CHRIST.

Look at your life right now. Do you have a personal relationship with Christ? Have you trusted Him as your Saviour? God will comfort you during this time, but you must have a personal relationship with Him. If you are skeptical of the fact that your loss would have anything to do with accepting Christ, consider one thing. Your loss caused you to pick up this book. It is in this book that you are reading about your need for a personal relationship with the Lord.

2.   IF YOU ARE AWAY FROM GOD, YOU HAVE THE OPPORTUNITY TO GET RIGHT WITH GOD.

I want to encourage you to look at your spiritual life right now. If you are a Christian, are you away from God? Was there a time when God had more of a priority in your life? If you have a broken relationship with God, this is the perfect time to mend it. You are going to need God more than ever through this journey. Do not continue to drift away from Him. Use your loss as an opportunity to renew your relationship with Him.

3.   YOU HAVE THE OPPORTUNITY TO DEEPEN YOUR RELATIONSHIP WITH GOD.

If you are a Christian and you have a good relationship with God, perhaps this is the opportunity that your loss is presenting. I believe through our loss we all have an opportunity to deepen our relationship with God. Again, grief is a spiritual matter.

During Amanda's hospital stays, there were many life and death situations. Many times the doctor would say that there was nothing more that he could do. I knew that I could call upon God. I prayed more during those times that Amanda was in the hospital than any other time in my life. I had to. I believe this excerpt from Chapter 5 from *An Angel Among Us* sums up this point fairly well.

As I stood over Amanda's bed while she was on the respirator, I knew that there was nothing that I could do to help her. As I watched each time that her breathing stopped and she had to be resuscitated, I knew that there was nothing that I could do. As I rubbed her head when she had a high fever, I knew that there was nothing that I could do. As my wife and I waited for crucial test results, I knew that there was nothing that I could do to make everything okay. In every ordeal that my wife and I watched our daughter suffer through, I knew that there was nothing that I could do.

Throughout all of the pain and suffering, God took my pride away. I had no answers or solutions. I had no more self-confidence. God had taken it all away. God had given me something to face that I knew that I had no chance of surviving on my own. He had put me in a situation in which I had to depend on someone other than myself.

For the first time in my life, I had to completely depend on God. I could not depend on past prayers or past victories. I had to depend on Him every moment of every day. Every day that passed, I had to depend on Him for strength. Often I would read Psalm 18:23 which says, "The Lord is my rock, and my fortress, and my deliverer; my God, my strength, in whom I will trust; my buckler, and the horn of my salvation, and my high tower." I realized very quickly that the only way that I would survive this trial would be to get strength from God.

Wherever you are in your spiritual life, your loss is going to give you spiritual opportunities. Will you take advantage of them? God loves us and wants to help us through these hard times.

SECTION TWO — GRIEF

6

Three Reasons Why Grief Destroys Lives

If you are going to survive your loss and the grief that accompanies it, you must understand that grief has the power to destroy your life. A common response to this statement is "My loss has already destroyed my life." Loss is hard to overcome, but grief makes your life unbearable. Grief is what reminds you every day of the fact you have lost. When you begin to cope with your loss, it is grief that causes the setbacks. When you begin to feel some happiness, it is grief that takes the joy and replaces it with sorrow. When you have "moved on", it is grief that takes you back to the graveside, the doctor's office, the divorce court, the empty crib, or some other place of loss. You must understand that grief has power. Loss has forever altered your life, but it is grief that has the potential to destroy your life.

> *Loss has forever altered your life, but it is grief that has the potential to destroy your life.*

THERE ARE THREE BASIC REASONS
GRIEF DESTROYS LIVES.

Each of these three reasons are simple yet crucial to preventing the grief of your loss from becoming the instrument that destroys all hope of recovery. Study these reasons with caution. The information found in this chapter may save your life.

I.   THE AVERAGE PERSON DOES NOT UNDERSTAND GRIEF.

You can not conquer what you can not understand. You can not prepare for what you do not know. You must study your opponent. Let me illustrate. I am a big Georgia Bulldog football fan. I celebrate every victory and lament every loss. I can name players and coaches. I know uniform numbers and years of remaining eligibility. In the off season, I follow recruiting and spring practice. During the season, I am attentive not only to the games but also to the practices and press conferences as well. During Coach Mark Richt's pregame press conference, he will refer to the fact that they are looking at the upcoming opponent on tape. He and the coaching staff do this to see the strengths and weaknesses of the future opponent. Mark Richt has been very successful as the coach at the University of Georgia. However, I guarantee you that he would not have the success he has had if he had not studied his opponents. You study your opponent to get an understanding of what you might face. I wish I could say Coach Richt had won every game he has coached, but sometimes the opponent gets the better of him in spite of his preparation. Sometimes your opponent gets the better of you too. By studying and preparing for your opponent, you are less likely to get defeated. Your opponent gets the better of you less often than if you had never prepared. Here is the lesson from this illustration. Some days grief will get the best of you. Grief will win. If you do not study and prepare for grief, grief will win every day. Study your opponent; he already knows how to beat you. I will explain this in detail in the next chapter.

II. THE AVERAGE PERSON DOES NOT REALIZE GRIEF.

The initial response to this statement usually is the question, "How can someone not know that they are grieving?". Let me explain. As a child, I heard the following illustration. If you want to boil a frog, you can not drop him in a pot of boiling water. He obviously feels the immediate pain and will jump out of the pot. If you want to boil a frog, you place him in water at room temperature. The frog will be content because he is comfortable. As you turn up the heat, the temperature of the water rises. The frog will sit in the water while he boils to death.

I never attempted this experiment to test its validity. However, it does illustrate the point I am trying to make. Our loss is like the frog dropped in the boiling water. It is immediate and sudden pain, and we want out. When we are grieving our loss, we are like the frog in the water that is room temperature. As our environment is changed because of grief, we become more uncomfortable. We are not sure why we are uncomfortable because the pot is not boiling. The effects of grief are taking their toll on us because we do not realize our grief. Many times people fail to "jump out of the pot" before it is too late.

GRIEF TIP
Does this scenario describe you? Is the environment that once was comfortable now feel uncomfortable because of grief? Analyze and note how grief has changed your environment.

There are several characteristics of people who do not realize grief. These are not the signs of grief that are discussed in a later chapter. These are attitudes and habits that people develop from not realizing they are grieving.

1.   THEY DO NOT UNDERSTAND THEIR LOSS.

These individuals have not grasped the fact that they have experienced loss. They do not have an obvious loss such as a loved one dying. Their loss would be along the lines of being abused as a child or experiencing some other form of loss where the person looks at himself as being the problem instead of the victim.

GRIEF TIP
Before you read any further, make sure you have identified your loss. You may want to refer to the chapters on loss and secondary loss before continuing reading. You can not recover from loss if you do not realize that you have lost.

2.   THEY TRY TO MINIMIZE THEIR LOSS.

"My loss is not a big deal." "I should be stronger than this." These are statements made by someone who does not realize his loss. I am for being strong. I am for having a positive approach to bad situations. However, you can not minimize your loss. Whatever your loss is, you must understand that it is a big deal. It has the power to not only alter your life but destroy it as well. I have had counseling appointments where the entire session was used to convince the individual that his loss was significant enough to grieve over. Once someone understands this, he can begin to deal with his grief.

GRIEF TIP

You must make your loss a big deal because others usually will minimize your loss. The more you minimize your loss, the less you feel you have a right to grieve.

---

3.   THEY TRY TO IGNORE IT.

A decaying tooth is not going to get better if you ignore it. It will continue to get worse and worse until you get it fixed, or the tooth completely decays, falls out, or causes infection. The quickest way to get someone to believe in a dentist who doesn't is for him to get a toothache. The quickest way for someone to believe in a chiropractor is for that person to hurt his back. The quickest way for an atheist to believe in God is for that person to face death. Likewise, the easiest way for a person to get help with his grief is to keep him from ignoring it.

GRIEF TIP
The more you ignore grief the more devastating grief is.

III.   MANY PEOPLE CAN NOT DEAL WITH THEIR GRIEF.

Of the three reasons that grief destroys lives listed in this chapter, I believe this reason is the one that destroys the most lives. I was in a store when I saw a woman that I had known for several years. It had been some time since I had seen her last. When I asked her how she was doing, she told me of some terrible losses that she was dealing with. During the course of the conversation, she made the statement that she could not deal with her grief. As big as her losses were, the truth is that she must deal with her grief. If she does not, it will destroy her. The scary reality is that this lady is not the only person I have ever encountered who felt like this. I can recall in my own life the desperate feeling of being overwhelmed by grief. Many times since my daughter's death, it seemed like grief had a stranglehold around my neck and had no intention of loosening its grip. I remember feeling this way before Amanda died as well. The ongoing struggle in the hospital also had me at a point of wondering if I could manage my grief.

> *Many times since my daughter's death, it seemed like grief had a stranglehold around my neck and had no intention of loosening its grip.*

The following excerpt of Chapter 9 in *An Angel Among Us* illustrates this part.

Now that Amanda had been taken off the ventilator, my wife and I were anticipating Amanda's recovery. She spent two more days in the Intensive Care Unit for observation. On New Year's Eve, we received word from the doctor that Amanda would be transferred to another floor. She would spend a few days there until the doctors felt she was strong enough to go home.

Needless to say, my wife and I were excited about the news. Even though we would not begin the new year at home, at least we would not be in the Intensive Care Unit any longer. After Amanda was transferred that evening, two doctors came in to introduce themselves to us. They explained that they would be caring for Amanda that night. We discussed her short history so they would know how to give her the best care possible.

As midnight approached, we decided to go down to the balcony and watch the fireworks over downtown Jacksonville. We were joined by my parents, and a few moments later the two doctors that had introduced themselves earlier. We spent a few minutes enjoying the evening before returning to Amanda's room. This was the first time in a couple of weeks that we had been able to relax and enjoy ourselves.

The next day was fairly eventful. The doctor had ordered a speech therapist to help with Amanda's feeding. It was so much fun getting to hold her during feedings. For a while we wondered if we would ever get to hold her again. The only thing that gave a cause for concern was the fact that Amanda had a fever. It lasted for most of the day, but the nurse told us she would check her temperature regularly.

During Amanda's first few days out of the Intensive Care Unit, the doctor discovered that she had a bladder infection. We were told that it would be treated with antibiotics. Amanda maintained a fever which caused us to have some concern, but we assumed that it had something to do with her bladder infection.

Early the next morning, I was awakened by the doctor. I had spent the night in Amanda's room while Heather went home to get some rest. The doctor told me that they had taken some of Amanda's blood for a test. The results of the test were cause for some concern. The white blood cell count was extremely high which indicated a serious infection. The doctor told me that they wanted to do a spinal tap to see if Amanda had meningitis. He told me that I could have a few minutes to think about this, and I would need to give my consent in order to have this procedure done.

The doctor left the room. I sat on the cot where I had been sleeping completely stunned. I never saw this coming. I had anticipated Amanda's full recovery, and now I am told that she may have meningitis. I put my head in my hands and began to cry. I was tired of the hospital and tired of seeing my daughter suffer. In a few minutes, the supervising doctor came into the room to tell me what the other doctor had already told me. I asked her how concerned I should be. She told me that I should be "very concerned". I asked her what she would do if Amanda were her child. She told me that she would have the spinal tap right away to rule out the possibility of meningitis. I told her to go ahead then and do it. A few minutes later the doctor whom I had spoken to earlier explained to me the risks involved in doing this procedure. I signed the consent form and waited for them to come to get Amanda.

I called my wife and told her everything that I had been told. I assured her that if I found out anything before she came to the hospital I would let her know. Shortly after I hung up the phone, a nurse came to get Amanda. I sat in the room alone wondering what would happen next. I prayed that the test results would come back negative. About twenty minutes had passed when the nurse brought Amanda back to the room. It broke my heart that she had to go through that. I told myself that there had to be a reason why God was allowing this to happen.

7

Understanding Grief

THREE THINGS TO UNDERSTAND ABOUT GRIEF

I. GRIEF IS NO RESPECTER OF PERSONS.

It does not matter who you are. Grief will find you at some point in your life. There is no one exempt from grief. On December 26, 2004, a tsunami devastated many parts of Thailand. This natural disaster took the lives of thousands of men, women, and children. This great wave of destruction made no discernment as to who would be a victim. It took the rich, the poor, the healthy, the sick, the young, and the old. Anyone on the beach that day was taken. Grief is much like that tsunami. It makes no difference who you are or what kind of life you live. If you have experienced loss, the tsunami of grief will devastate you.

II. GRIEF IS NECESSARY.

There are many unpleasant but necessary things that we must do in our lives. I do not like going to the dentist. I can think of so many other things that I would rather do than sit in a dentist's chair. However, when I have a toothache, going to the dentist does not sound as bad to me because it is necessary. Grief is much the same way. No one wants to grieve, but grief is necessary to get relief from your loss.

Many show they do not understand grief because they do not realize the necessity of grief. You must grieve after a loss. Grief is the bridge that connects loss to recovery.

GRIEF TIP
Do not fight your natural impulse to grieve. It is much simpler to embrace it.

III.   GRIEF IS DIFFICULT.

The third real evidence that many do not understand grief is the failure to understand the fact that grief is difficult. This is the breaking point for some people. Take a look at this scenario. A woman in her late thirties loses her husband to a horrible car accident. She is now left to rear her three young children by herself. Her financial stability is also gone. She can barely manage the pain from this great loss. After experiencing this great tragedy, she now must go through a period of emotional distress and pain. This is a difficult reality.

Many people make the mistake of underestimating the pain and difficulty of grief. This is evidence of their lack of understanding. This does not mean the grieving person is dumb or naive. Grief is something that we do not educate ourselves on, and we hope we never will need to.

8

Why Some Can Not Deal with Grief

I believe there are three main reasons why some can not deal with grief. This section will be a help to you by revealing why you can not deal with grief. As you read through these reasons, make a point to try to identify how they relate to you.

1.   THE ROLLER COASTER OF GRIEF IS HARD TO HANDLE.

If you have ever been to an amusement park, usually the most imposing structure is the roller coaster. The things that make a roller coaster a roller coaster are the steep climbs and the big drops. The higher the climb, the farther the ride will drop. The farther the ride drops, the greater the thrill. In the day we live in, the more extreme the roller coaster, the more people want to ride it. Today's roller coaster will drop you, twist you, put you on the verge of losing your lunch, and have you screaming for more.

Grief is like a roller coaster ride in that it has many ups and downs. You have moments that would be considered "highs." A good example of a high would be when friends and family rush to your side, and it is revealed to you how much people love you. There are also many "lows" in the roller coaster of grief. Times when you are alone or faced with questions that you can not answer would be an example of a low.

Just like on a roller coaster, the higher the "highs," the greater the drops or "lows" will be. Unlike the ride in an amusement park, the "roller coaster of grief" is no fun. We know grief is hard. If you are on this "grief roller coaster" you can relate to the difficulty that I am describing.

I have ridden many roller coasters. On numerous occasions there has been someone screaming that he wants to get off the ride. On one occasion, the ride was stopped so a frantic rider could be taken off of the ride. Many times "riders" of the "grief roller coaster" decide they want off of this crazy ride. Unfortunately, there is no park attendant to stop the ride to get them off when they are frantic. There is no way to get off the "grief roller coaster." You must finish the ride.

For some, the fact they must finish the ride is not something that they accept. Then, unfortunately, lives are devastated by bad decisions. The "rider" says, "If I can not get off of the 'roller coaster,' then I will do whatever is necessary to forget about the 'roller coaster'." This kind of rationale is a life destroyer. This rationale is a marriage destroyer. Where does one possibly turn to forget about grief. Many people have become alcoholics who have refused to ride the "roller coaster of grief." Many people have become drug addicts because they refused to ride the "roller coaster of grief." Some have even ended their life because they could no longer ride the "roller coaster of grief."

It may not be drugs or alcohol or suicide. For some it might be alienating loved ones, bitterness, quitting a job, or giving up on life. The "roller coaster of grief" is hard enough by itself. Do not make it harder by having to fight an addiction while dealing with your loss, or put yourself in a position where you must deal with loss by yourself.

GRIEF TIP
A roller coaster ride is scarier when you ride by yourself than when you ride with other people. Keep as close as you can to as many people as you can while on the "roller coaster of grief."

2.   SOME DO NOT TAKE ACTION.

Those who refuse to take action following their loss will be overwhelmed by their grief. I stressed the importance of taking action in Chapter 2. I commend you for reading this far. It is more than likely that the fact that you have continued to read is evidence that you have decided to take action following your loss. Do not stop reading, and do not stop applying the things you learn from this book. Those who enter the aftermath of loss and approach grief with the attitude that they can not overcome these unfortunate things in their life do not overcome loss and grief.

3.   SOME DO NOT EQUIP THEMSELVES FOR
        GRIEF.

The look on the face of someone who has had a loss gives away the fact he has not equipped himself for grief. How do I equip myself for grief? Is there some sort of grief kit I can purchase? I have never heard of that before. These are statements I have been approached with after making the statement that we must equip ourselves for grief. I have never seen a "grief prevention kit" for sale anywhere I have ever shopped, but it is possible to equip ourselves for grief.

There are three things we should incorporate in our lives that will equip us for grief.

A. FAITH

Perhaps you have seen the bumper sticker that reads "He who has the most toys wins." The reality is: He who has the most faith wins. The importance of faith can not be underestimated. Grief puts us in a situation where we can not depend on ourselves. It becomes increasingly important to depend on a higher power.

> *Show me a person with no faith, and I will show you a person that will be devastated by grief.*

My faith in God is what sustains me. During the hardest times of my daughter's struggles, it was God Who kept me going. During the lowest times following my daughter's death, it was God Who kept me going. Show me a person with no faith, and I will show you a person that will be devastated by grief. It is necessary to be a person of faith if you are to be properly equipped for grief.

B.   OTHERS

If you are to be properly equipped, you must depend on others. You can not make it through the journey of heartache alone. Surround yourself with positive people. Surround yourself with caring people. Also surround yourself with encouraging people. There is an old saying, "Birds of a feather flock together." If you are around negative people, you will be negative. If you are around selfish people, you will be selfish. Because someone is a family member or a life-long friend does not mean he is the right person for you to be around while grieving. Those who surround you will directly impact your journey through grief. Make sure you choose wisely.

GRIEF TIP
Analyze the people who you spend the most time with. Are they good for your grief?

C.   TOOLS

Along with faith and others, it is important that we are equipped with the right tools. A carpenter must have the right tools. It would not be fair to expect him to frame a house with landscaping tools. Likewise, we can not expect ourselves to travel the journey through grief without being equipped with the right tools. Here are a few things to equip yourself with for your journey.

Bible	Books	Quotes
Poems	Inspirational Songs	Encouraging Letters

Use the following chart to remind you of what you need to equip yourself.

How do you equip yourself for the journey through heartache?
Right Strength = Faith
Right People = Others
Right Help = Tools

GRIEF TIP
Copy this chart and place it where you will see it often.

9

Signs of Grief

I have had the same family physician for more than twenty years. Fortunately, I have not had to call on him very many times. However, there have been a few occasions that I had to see him. After I sign in, I sit and wait until the doctor is ready to see me. A nurse eventually calls my name and escorts me into the office area. The routine usually begins with getting my weight, then ushering me into a room where the nurse takes my blood pressure. I am then informed that the doctor will be in to see me soon. After the doctor comes in and says hello, the questioning begins. "How do you feel?" "Where is the pain coming from?" "How long have you felt this way?" He listens to my answers usually while scribbling something on my chart, then he makes his diagnosis. Next, he prescribes whatever medicines deal with whatever sickness I have. It is not uncommon for more than one medicine to be prescribed. Sometimes one medicine will treat the symptoms while another will treat the sickness.

As you were reading the last paragraph, you probably were picturing your last doctor's visit. The scene I described was probably very similar to your experience. Perhaps, your doctor asked the same questions. Regardless of what questions he asked, your doctor did ask some questions. Why did he ask those questions? Before a doctor can make a diagnosis, he must know the symptoms. (If your doctor makes a diagnosis without knowing any symptoms, you might want to find a new doctor.) When you experience loss, you must check the signs of grief before you can make a diagnosis of recovery. These signs will help you understand that you are grieving. Before you can take your "medicine," you must accept the diagnosis. Many people do not recover from loss because they do not understand, or they do not accept that they are grieving. Someone who is vomiting, has a high fever, and body aches probably has a good idea that he has the flu. This person could deny having the flu even though all of the signs say that he does. The mistake many grieving people make is that they deny the fact they are grieving although all of the signs say that they are.

> When you experience loss, you must check the signs of grief before you can make a diagnosis of recovery.

> The mistake many grieving people make is that they deny the fact they are grieving although all of the signs say that they are.

Grief can be recognized. If you are reading this book because you have experienced loss, the signs mentioned in this chapter will put many things into perspective for you. If you are reading this book because you know someone who has experienced loss, the signs mentioned in this chapter will help you recognize the grief that he is dealing with. Perhaps, you can be a great help to the one who has lost by getting him to understand exactly what he is dealing with.

SIGN #1- EXHAUSTION

Any time that your emotions are involved in a situation, you will be affected by being physically tired. We have all heard the terms "emotionally spent," or "emotionally drained." When we experience loss, our emotions are taken to the extreme. These emotions of hurt and sadness become the center point of our feelings. Many times, we are not aware of how this wears on our body physically. Through a loss, we can be at the mercy of our emotions for many days, weeks, months, or even years. Our bodies can be very resilient, but eventually get to the point of exhaustion.

Along with our emotions wearing on us, our sleeping schedule usually changes during a period of loss. When we have a loved one die, we become too busy dealing with the loss by making arrangements, calling loved ones, etc., that we do not take the time to rest. Any type of loss usually keeps us from resting because of the many things that we deal with mentally, physically, and emotionally. Our body eventually reaches the point of exhaustion.

There are three common reasons why we physically reach the point of exhaustion.

1.   WE DO NOT GET GOOD REST.

This is rest where our mind and body truly slow down and relax.

2.   WE DO NOT GET ENOUGH REST.

We fail to understand that because our emotions are pushed to the extreme, we need more physical rest.

3.   WE DO NOT GET UNINTERRUPTED REST.

We do not have an extended period of time when our body can "shut down." Our rest time is interrupted because of a change in schedule, new responsibilities, change of surroundings, preoccupied mind, etc.

GRIEF TIP
Set aside time every day to rest. Even a thirty-minute nap will make a big difference.

SIGN #2 - DISTRACTION

When we experience loss, our mind becomes occupied with many things. Besides dealing with our everyday lives, we now are forced to sort through issues mentally. What makes this especially difficult is that now we must deal mentally and emotionally with things that we have no desire to deal with. Our mind becomes occupied with what is now priority, and we are unable to concentrate on other things.

We also get distracted because there are many things that "trigger" our emotions. You can be at work engrossed in accomplishing your responsibilities when you hear a word, phrase, or expression used by a co-worker that immediately reminds you of your loss. You can see something in a store or a product advertisement on TV that reminds you of your loss. This will cause memories and emotions to come back to you. When this happens, you are distracted from the task at hand. Just because you are able to be "back at work" does not mean you are really "back to work."

KEYS TO NOT GETTING DISTRACTED

KEY #1 - DO NOT PLACE TOO MUCH ON YOURSELF.

The magnitude of your loss depends on the amount you can place on yourself. I do not wish to minimize any loss, but all losses are not equal. The greater the loss, the less we can handle.

When we are grieving, many times we must place our dreams and ambitions on hold. Our responsibilities are difficult enough to keep under control. We must realize that while we are grieving, we are not capable of doing all of the things that we would like to do.

> We must realize that while we are grieving, we are not capable of doing all of the things that we would like to do.

KEY #2 - LOWER YOUR EXPECTATIONS.

While grieving, you must not expect too much of yourself. When we try to do too much too soon, we frustrate ourselves because it is not possible to do all that we did before. How foolish would it be for me to lose a child and believe that I was able to do everything that I did before Amanda died. I tried to jump into the same schedule that I had before Amanda was sick. I had a full teaching schedule, and a full speaking schedule, among other responsibilities. It did not take me long to figure out that I could not keep this schedule. I was really disappointed in myself because I could not effectively do all the things I had previously done. This was due to distraction. I could not focus on every responsibility; therefore, my ability to do any of my responsibilities was affected.

There are three things to keep in mind concerning lowering your expectations while grieving.

1.   YOU PROBABLY CAN NOT DO EVERYTHING THAT YOU DID BEFORE.

2.   YOU PROBABLY CAN NOT DO EVERYTHING YOU WANT TO DO.

3.   YOU PROBABLY CAN NOT DO EVERYTHING THAT YOU NEED TO DO.

GRIEF TIP
Focus on one thing at a time. Accomplish or deal with one task before you move on to the next.

SIGN # 3 – PHYSICAL CHANGES

Before Amanda died, the part of grief that I was the most ignorant about was the physical effects that grief would cause. However, the affect grief has on your health is very real. How much grief affects your health depends on a couple of factors. The two determining factors are how great was your loss and how strong was your health before your loss. If your loss is comparatively small, and your health is good; there probably will not be a great change in your health. However, if your loss is great and your health is poor, the physical effects of grief can be devastating. Look at the illustration of these factors.

TWO EXTREMES

Comparatively small loss + good health = little effect
Great loss + poor health = potentially devastating effect

Take a look at your situation. All loss is big to the one who has lost. Comparatively speaking, have you experienced a small loss or a great loss? Analyze your health before your loss. Was it good health or poor health? These factors will make a difference in how many and by what magnitude you are affected by the physical symptoms listed on the next page.

Use the following self-evaluation exercise to determine where you fall in the two extremes concerning your loss and your health. Use the number one to signify the smallest loss and the best health. Use the number ten to signify the greatest loss and the poorest health. Circle the number that best describes your loss and your health before your loss. Add the two numbers together. The closer to twenty you are the more devastating the physical effects will be.

LOSS

| 1 | 2 | 3 | 4 | 5 | 6 | 7 | 8 | 9 | 10 |

HEALTH

| 1 | 2 | 3 | 4 | 5 | 6 | 7 | 8 | 9 | 10 |

The following is a list of some common physical changes.

1. Sleep Difficulties
2. Appetite Change (Weight Loss or Gain)
3. Numbness
4. Frequent Headaches
5. Physically Weak – No Stamina
6. Disoriented and Forgetful

GRIEF TIP

Eat as healthy as possible and get some exercise and rest.

SIGN #4 – ANGER

Experiencing loss combined with the many different aspects of grief is a perfect combination for anger. Anger is generally an easy sign to spot. Usually, we do not confuse our anger with another emotion. It is an easy emotion for others to see in us also. This result of grief is potentially devastating if we do not give it the attention that it deserves.

The following lists were compiled from my own

experiences along with information I received through counseling with many who are grieving. Perhaps every entry does not apply to you, but hopefully this will be a guide and a help in dealing with anger caused by grief. **At the end of each list, space has been provided for you to fill in those things that apply to you but are not listed.**

WHY WE GET ANGRY

1. We feel others are not as sympathetic to our loss as they should be.
2. We feel others should be more sensitive to our needs.
3. Others move on with their lives when we can not.
4. Others do not remember your loss.
5. We get angry that this happened to us instead of someone else.
6. We disappoint ourselves.
7. We are irritable.
8. We have an inability to focus.
9. Others have what we no longer have.
10. We feel as though a loved one left us.
11. _____
12. _____
13. _____
14. _____
15. _____

WHAT TO DO WHEN WE GET ANGRY

1. Take a breath.
2. Take a walk.
3. Read the Bible.
4. Pray for help in dealing with your anger and your loss.
5. Find a private and safe place to vent your anger.
6. Write out your feelings on paper.
7. Reflect on positive memories.
8. _____
9. _____
10. _____
11. _____
12. _____

SIGN #5 – UNCERTAINTY

I am an ambitious person. I have big dreams and big goals. If you were to ask me where I was going in life at the age of twenty-five, I could have told you. I had life all planned out. If you asked me where I was going in life at the age of twenty-seven, I did not have any idea. The reason for the change in two short years was the struggle and death of my daughter, Amanda. Grief destroys some dreams while it puts others on hold. Even now I am uncertain about many aspects of the future. Do not be alarmed if you are uncertain about things in the future. This is a sign that you are grieving. This happens when we have experienced loss. Grief takes what was once certain and makes it uncertain.

> Grief takes what was once certain and makes it uncertain.

GRIEF TIP

When you are facing uncertainty because of loss, concentrate on the constants of your life. List a few things that are constant in your life. Refer to this list during the uncertain times of your life.

SIGN #6 – FEAR

Including Amanda, God has blessed me with three beautiful daughters. Because of the experience with Amanda, I live with fear. I am afraid that my daughters will get seriously ill. I know that it can happen because I have experienced it. I am afraid that something horrible could happen to my daughters that may take their life. I know that it can happen. There are two types of fear that are considered signs of grief. The first is the fear of the unknown, and the second is the fear of the things we can not control.

I believe there is a key principle to understanding and dealing with the fears that come from grief. Your greatest loss becomes your greatest fear. Memorize this statement. Write it where you will see it often. It will help you through the fears that come from grieving.

In my life, my greatest fear was losing a child. This fear developed after Amanda died. I have counseled with several people whose parents divorced while they were a child. There was a common fear of divorce in their own marriage. When someone is abused as a child, it is not uncommon for him to fear that happening to his own children. If you have a parent die, it is probable that your great fear will be that of losing your living parent.

GRIEF TIP
Let your greatest fear become your greatest strength. Since I had a child die, I do not take for granted a single day with my other children. I am motivated to be the best father that I can possibly be.

GRIEF TIP
Determine how you can turn your greatest fear into your greatest strength.

SIGN #7 – DISCONNECTED FROM REALITY

It is no secret that loss and grief change our life. Grief disorients us and causes emotional confusion. While we are grieving, we must understand that the world does keep turning. Many times, it is very difficult to stay in touch with reality. The grieving person either takes things too seriously or not seriously enough.

REASONS THE GRIEVING PERSON IS DISCONNECTED FROM REALITY.

WITHDRAW SOCIALLY

While we are grieving, we do not want to interact with people. We do not know how to nor do we have the desire to socialize with other people. This is a completely normal reaction caused by our hurt.

IMPULSIVE

Do not make any important decisions without giving them much thought. It is common to not think things through and weigh all of the consequences. It might be a good idea to leave your checkbook and credit cards at home. Since we can not have back something that we want, making a decision on impulse allows us to be satisfied by "getting something we want." Unfortunately, we can get ourselves into financial trouble because we made a decision on impulse.

> Since we can not have back something that we want, making a decision on impulse allows us to be satisfied by "getting something we want."

IF?

If I had done things differently. If he had not driven that night. If we had made a different decision. Allowing the word *if* to enter our thought process keeps us from reality. The word *if* can not change or reverse what has already happened.

NOT OBJECTIVE

We are unable to make a decision without it being prejudiced by our loss. It would be abnormal for us to make decisions freely without referencing our grief. Many times, decisions are made based on what makes us feel better as opposed to what is best.

GRIEF TIP

Recruit a group of trusted advisers to rely on for help making decisions. Keep in mind family and close friends are usually grieving your loss as well, so they may not be the best choices.

SIGN #8 – DREAMS

I remember when Amanda was alive actually dreaming that she passed away. After Amanda died, I took my family on a trip. While we were on this trip, I dreamed that Amanda was alive. I have dreamed many times that Amanda was not an infant but a little girl. I do not claim to be an expert on why people have dreams. However, I do know that grief occupies every part of you, especially your mind. When you sleep, your mind is still occupied with that which consumes your thoughts. Sometimes my dreams would be very disturbing to me. What helped me was the understanding that this was not uncommon because I was grieving the loss of something very important to me.

When I travel with my wife, sometimes I am faced with a question that all men hate to hear. "Do you know where you are going?" Out of the corner of my eye I check the road signs. Then as all men do, I answer with an emphatic, "Yes!" It really does not matter how I answer because the signs reveal exactly where I am. I have a few questions for you that the grieving individual does not like to hear. Are you okay? How are you dealing with your loss? Are you grieving? Before you answer, check the signs.

10

The Stages and Phases of Grief

I frequently receive calls from families who have experienced the loss of a child. I met Ray and Angie, Wilvern and Omega, and Will and Shelly all in one year's time. All of these couples had lost a child. All three couples were grieving. Although they had grief in common, it was not hard to understand that they were in different places on their journey.

In order to fully understand the grieving process, the grieving person must understand that there are different stages of grief. The grieving person must also understand that in those different stages one will pass through different phases of grief. The phases of grief that you deal with will help you determine the stage of grief that you are in.

GRIEF TIP
As you read this chapter, determine what stage you are in currently.

I. SURVIVAL STAGE

The stage in which you feel the greatest number

of different emotions is the survival stage. What is the survival stage? It is exactly what the name says that it is–survival. Your goal is to make it through the day. Your goal tomorrow is to make it through another day. You can not see down the road. Today is almost too much to handle. Life is just about survival in this stage. This is the stage the grieving person lives in immediately following their loss.

GRIEF TIP
While you are in the survival stage, do not try to survive and succeed, or survive and excel. Simply surviving will be challenge enough.

PHASE ONE – SHOCK

I was sitting in the hospital waiting room with Mrs. Linda Crews. Mrs. Crews is the mother of a classmate whom I graduated from high school with. We were in the hospital waiting room because earlier in the day, Stephanie had been in a serious car accident. We were there for some time when the doctor came into the room. He sat directly in front of Mrs. Crews and told her the grim news that Stephanie was at the point of death and there was nothing more that the doctors could do. He informed her that Stephanie would pass away very soon.

I will never forget the initial look on Mrs. Crews' face. She sat in front of the doctor in shock. It was very obvious that she had not expected such terrible news.

The phase of shock hits all of us when we experience loss. I believe it is an accurate statement to say the phase of shock triggers grief. You may not be grieving the loss of a loved one because of a tragic loss, but you are shocked with the reality of loss at some point. It might be the realization that your marriage is over, or the report you receive from the doctor. If you are grieving, at some point you have experienced shock.

PHASE TWO – DENIAL

I remember receiving the news that Amanda would not live very long. After the initial shock, I remember telling myself that there had to be some kind of mistake. I told myself that she would get better, and that she would live longer than the doctors thought. Although I had seen the results of Amanda's tests, I still denied what I had been told. Do you refuse to accept the reality of life's losses? Do you refuse to accept the possibility that the worst thing that could happen has happened or will happen?

GRIEF TIP
Do not confuse optimism and denial. Being optimistic is believing good could happen; denial is refusing that bad could happen.

PHASE THREE – BLAME

When we experience loss, we grieve. Grieving is an emotional roller coaster filled with pain. When we have lost a loved one, marriage, job, etc., we lose things that we did not wish to give up. When this happens, we look for something or someone to blame for our unfortunate circumstances.

GRIEF TIP
Remember loss occurs because it is part of life. Do not hurt yourself or others by placing blame where it does not belong.

PHASE FOUR – ANGER

Anger is an emotion we experience when we feel that life has wronged us. My baby should not have died. My marriage should not have ended. My parents should not have divorced. I should not have been abused. All of these statements may seem true to us, but unfortunately in life things happen that are very unfair. Anger is a common reaction. Anger is a built-in emotion that is triggered by many things. It is not uncommon after reality sets in to become angry because of what life has dealt us. Let us take a look at whom we direct our anger during these trying times.

> Anger is an emotion we experience when we feel that life has wronged us.

- God
- Ourselves
- One who caused the loss (one who died, one who filed for divorce, the one who left, etc.)
- Loved ones
- Doctors and nurses
- Strangers

Although anger is a natural emotion, it is an emotion that must be controlled. Anger will control you.

Anger will alter your judgment. Anger will make you bitter.

GRIEF TIP
Determine not to direct your anger at anyone. "Venting" may allow temporary relief but might cause long-term damage.

PHASE FIVE – GUILT

Guilt is a phase that many people spend a long time in. We feel guilty because we convince ourselves that we could have prevented the loss in our life. I believe there are two main reasons why those who are grieving feel guilt.

1.   YOU FEEL THAT YOU COULD HAVE OR SHOULD HAVE DONE SOMETHING DIFFERENT.

When Amanda was alive, I remember many times being tired and frustrated with the care that she had to have. I felt guilty many times for getting frustrated or allowing myself to get tired. I have felt guilty for not doing more for her when she was alive.

2.   FEELING HAPPINESS AFTER THE LOSS.

One misnomer of grief is that you can never experience joy or happiness while grieving. Guilt creeps in whenever we experience a light moment after our loss.

GRIEF TIP
Hindsight fuels our guilt. We can not change what has happened. We only torture ourselves by looking back at what could be different.

PHASE SIX – DEPRESSION AND LONELINESS

One of the unfortunate affects of the survival stage is loneliness. You might be around people or have gone back to work, but you still feel lonely. It is natural for grief to cause you to withdraw yourself from conversation and fellowship.

This loneliness accentuates the feelings of "Life is over." Depression is brought on by an inability "to resume business as normal." Even though we feel alone in this situation, it is important not to be alone in this situation.

GRIEF TIP
Even though you do not want to interact with people at this point, make yourself be around people. Make yourself walk around a mall or another place where there are a large number of people.

II.   THE RECOVERY STAGE

The recovery stage is the next stage you find yourself in after experiencing loss. In this stage, you begin to recover from your loss. This is the stage where you transition from mere survival to beginning to live again. Those in this stage have experienced the

> Recovery is not going back to the way that it was before your loss. Recovery is beginning to find meaning to life again.

previously mentioned phases of shock, denial, blame, anger, guilt, and loneliness. Recovery is not going back to the way that it was before your loss. Recovery is beginning to find meaning to life again.

The recovery stage is an easier stage to deal with. Bear in mind that no stage is easy. However, this stage is easier to deal with on a daily basis. Read carefully the following phases to learn how to move into the recovery stage.

PHASE ONE – ACCEPTING REALITY

Accepting reality keeps many people out of the recovery stage. You can not begin to recover unless you are able to accept what has happened in your life. Acceptance is the opposite of denial mentioned in the previous stage.

After Amanda passed away, there were many things my wife and I had to deal with. One of which was reality. Shortly, after Amanda's death, we decided to pack her room. We packed her clothes and nursery decorations. We kept a few mementos, but we got rid of everything else. We painted the walls and turned her room into a playroom for my oldest daughter. This did not mean we were trying to forget Amanda: it meant we were accepting the loss of Amanda. I must emphasize that we did not do this until we were ready; but as soon as we felt we were ready, we undertook this painful task.

If you were to walk through our house, you would see many pictures and reminders of Amanda. We have not forgotten her, but we have accepted the loss of her presence. You must come to terms with your loss. Failure to accept your loss is keeping you from recovery. If you have gone through a divorce, you must accept it. If you were abused as a child, you must accept it. If you have lost a loved one, you must accept it. If you have lost your health, you must accept it. You must accept your loss as part of your life before you can recover.

GRIEF TIP
Determine whether or not you have accepted your loss. If you have not accepted your loss, do so now so that you may recover.

PHASE TWO – ALLOWING YOURSELF TO HURT

Loss brings pain. Adjusting to loss means adjusting to the pain. You must allow yourself to hurt. No person in his or her right mind enjoys pain. Pain is a normal reaction. When we refuse to hurt, we are refusing ourselves a necessary and normal response.

You must accept your loss before you enter the recovery stage. By accepting your loss, you are accepting the pain that accompanies the loss. When you allow yourself to hurt, you are allowing yourself to recover. This helps you move into the next phase of the recovery stage.

PHASE THREE – ADJUSTING TO LIFE AFTER LOSS

You are truly recovering when you adjust to life after your loss. The divorcee adjusts to being single again. The mother who loses a child adjusts to not being a mother to that child. The man or woman who loses a spouse adjusts to life after the death of that loved one. Whatever the loss in your life is, to recover, you must adjust to life after the loss.

Please bear in mind that I did not say the grieving person likes this adjustment. However, to recover this person must adjust. While you were grieving, the world kept moving. Grief caused you to change, but did not change the people around you. You must adjust to the differences in your new world caused by grief.

PHASE FOUR – FINDING NEW PURPOSE

Finding a new purpose is an obvious sign that you are in the recovery stage. This is the phase where you quit existing and begin living again. Your loss might have taken your motivation away from you. When you are truly recovering, you find new motivation.

GRIEF TIP
Try to determine what purpose you now have. Write down what your new purpose is and keep it where you can see it daily.

III.   THE REFLECTING STAGE

This is the last stage of grief. This stage is entered after the grieving person has been through the previous stages and phases. The reflecting stage is the stage after loss where the grieving person can look back on the grieving experience from the point of loss until the present. This is the stage when we are able to look back and evaluate all that we have been through. We are able to reflect on all of the emotions we have encountered, all the fears and uncertainties we have faced, as well as evaluate lessons that we have learned. With this information in mind, read the phases that you encounter in this stage.

PHASE ONE – FORGIVENESS

Throughout the whole grief process, there are probably people who offended you or hurt you in some way. You are now at the point to forgive them. Most people had no intentions of hurting you and probably do not even know that they have hurt you. At this point, the person who is in need of your forgiveness the most is you. You must forgive yourself. The following are things that we need to forgive ourselves for:

- Contributing to the loss
- Not somehow preventing the loss
- Not doing things differently before the loss
- How you responded to the loss
- How you treated others since the loss
- The emotions you felt while grieving
- Not responding better to the loss
- Poor decisions made while grieving
- Our failures since the loss

This of course is not an exclusive list. Hopefully,

this list caused you to look at yourself and see the different things that you need to forgive yourself for. No one is perfect. No one is without mistake. This is especially true while you are grieving.

GRIEF TIP
Make a list of all the areas of your life where you need to forgive yourself. Use this as a checklist until you have completely forgiven yourself of all shortcomings that were a result of your loss.

PHASE TWO – REMEMBERING

"Out of sight, out of mind." I believe this is how many live in the survival and recovery stage. Remembering brings back all the pain and heartache. In this final stage, you can remember the loss without losing control of your emotions. I can now look back and remember Amanda. Although she lived a short and difficult life, there are some good memories to reflect on.

When death takes a loved one, there are many difficult days to face. The loved one's birthday, the wedding anniversary, or the anniversary of his or her death are all hard days. Immediately following Amanda's death, I began to dread the arrival of her birthday that was just a few short months away. That first birthday was very hard to deal with. On her birthday now, even though it is still a difficult day, I am able to reminisce about the life of my daughter not the loss of my daughter. This day is now an opportunity for me to honor her memory as opposed to being just a reminder that she is gone.

"Time heals all wounds." I am sure you have probably heard this statement before. I do not believe this to be a true statement. Time will not bring my daughter back, nor will it fill the void in my life. However, time will allow us to reflect on the good memories that are associated with our loss.

There are several things to remember about these three stages.

1. Everyone goes through these stages at different speeds.
2. You might spend a longer time in a stage than someone else who is grieving.
3. Do not attempt to hurry through one of these stages. You can not. You will move to the next stage when you are ready.
4. When you move to another stage, it does not mean you will not feel the things you felt in the previous stage. Moving into the recovery stage will not exempt you from feeling anger, shock, guilt, blame, or loneliness.

GRIEF TIP
Determine what stage you are in now. Concentrate on the different phases associated with that stage. Do this for all three stages.

11

How Grief Affects Relationships

Everyone knows that losing someone we love has a great affect on us. One area that we are impacted is in our relationships. It is very important for the grieving person to understand that everything changes when he experiences loss, even relationships. I have talked to many people who were dealing with the loss in their life but could not deal with their existing relationships. From my experience in dealing with people who have experienced loss, this is common. It is important to understand that grief has a positive and negative affect on relationships. Some of your relationships will be affected in a positive way, while some are affected in a negative way. As you read this chapter, you may find that some of your relationships are stronger in some ways but weaker in others. The affect that grief has on relationships is different for each person. Let us consider how relationships are affected.

I.   GRIEF STRENGTHENS EXISTING RELATIONSHIPS.

    A.   GRIEF STRENGTHENS THE HUSBAND/ WIFE RELATIONSHIP.

In my particular case, my wife and I had to care for Amanda several months before she passed away. We faced every trial together. Even though we dealt with things differently, we still climbed every mountain together. After caring for Amanda for so long and then experiencing the loss in our lives, we depended on each other very much. Our love for each other was made stronger because we went through this heartache together. While we were both grieving, we would encourage each other. When I was having a particularly bad day, she would encourage me. Likewise I would encourage her during her hard times.

Another reason our relationship was strengthened was the fact that we were the ones feeling the greatest loss. Amanda was our child. Although others were saddened by her death, my wife and I were the parents who had lost a child. Grief strengthens the husband and wife relationship.

B.   GRIEF STRENGTHENS THE PARENT/ CHILD RELATIONSHIP.

I have met several people who are testimony to this. I know of one man who after his mother passed away mended an estranged relationship with his father. I have had several people comment that they were close to their parents before; but since they have gone through the grieving process, they are much closer to their parents now. I can certainly say this is true in my case.

As a parent who has lost a child, I feel that I now have a greater love for my children. Certainly, I loved my children before, but I now know what it is like to lose a child. I have experienced the horrible pain, as well as the overwhelming grief of knowing that my child has passed away. If you have grieved over the loss of a child, then certainly you understand how special your children are. It is not something we readily realize, but grief has caused us to love our other children more.

C.   THE RELATIONSHIPS BETWEEN
        SIBLINGS ARE STRENGTHENED.

I have talked with several people who have made statements such as: "I'm glad I had my brother to go through this with." "If I had not had my sister, I never would have made it." It is natural for a brother or a sister to come to the aid of a sibling, and there is no greater time to do this than when they are grieving. I understand that not every brother and sister can or will be there in the time of need for many reasons. However, the ones that are able to offer support have their relationships strengthened.

We must also look at this from the perspective of someone who has lost a sibling. It is obviously devastating to lose a sibling at any age. It does not matter if the sibling is a playmate, has his own family, or has lived a long, full life. Losing a sibling is hard to deal with.

When Amanda died, I obviously was concerned with how my wife and I would deal with the loss. I also was greatly concerned with how my three year old daughter, Alyssa, would take Amanda's death as well. Alyssa loved having a sister. I will never forget coming home from the hospital and explaining why Amanda's crib was empty.

It was no fun task to explain that Amanda would not be coming home. Alyssa took the news like I suppose any three year old would. She missed her sister.

As time passed, Alyssa constantly talked about having another sister. My wife and I were both very excited to tell Alyssa that she would have another sister. God blessed us with another beautiful girl, Anna. Alyssa adores Anna. She showers her with hugs and kisses. Even though there is a five year difference between them, Alyssa loves to play with her sister. Alyssa has asked me on more than one occasion, "Does Anna have to go to Heaven too?" Even as a small child, Alyssa understands what it is like to grieve in her own way. It is obvious to me that Alyssa loves Anna more because she lost Amanda.

> It is obvious to me that Alyssa loves Anna more because she lost Amanda.

D. GRIEF ALSO HAS A STRENGTHENING AFFECT ON THE FRIEND RELATIONSHIP.

"I never would have made it without a friend like you." What a powerful statement! I believe a true friend is someone who is there for you during the hard times of life. To be able to lean on a friend during times of grief is truly a Godsend.

During our time of heartache, my wife and I had many friends we could count on. There were many acts of kindness as well as selflessness shown to us by our friends. Even though some friend's acts were very brief, I felt a stronger bond toward them because of it. One example of this is how I feel toward those who took time to send flowers or come to my daughter's funeral. Those acts make me feel very close to them. Short phone calls or an occasional note not only were encouraging, but also deepened our feelings toward those who sent the note or made the call. I have friends whom I was not very close to; but after they helped me during my grieving, I feel very close to now. Likewise, I have had people whom I have helped through their grieving who have expressed their strong feelings toward me. Grief puts you in a situation where you need a friend, and allows others to be a friend to you.

E.   GRIEF WILL ALSO STRENGTHEN THE PASTOR/CHURCH MEMBER RELATIONSHIP.

I realize that not everyone reading this book will have a pastor or be a part of a church. If you are one of those people refer to Chapter 5, "How Loss Affects You Spiritually" and find you a church to be a part of.

For those readers who are fortunate enough to have a pastor to call upon, you will find that your relationship with him will strengthen while you are grieving. This is a natural thing. Your pastor was probably one of the first people you called when your loved one passed away. In the case of a long-term illness, it was your pastor whom you depended on for prayer.   It was your pastor who helped you make the funeral arrangements, and probably did the funeral service as well. It is now through your pastor's preaching that you get the strength you need. I have had many people express how much closer they feel to their pastor since he was there to comfort them in their time of grief.

II.   GRIEF WEAKENS EXISTING RELATIONSHIPS.

It is important to understand that the chaos that your life becomes when you lose someone you love is going to have a negative affect in some way. Just as sure as grief strengthens relationships, it certainly has the power to weaken them as well. In order to stop this from happening, we must first understand that it does happen.

A.   GRIEF WEAKENS THE HUSBAND/WIFE RELATIONSHIP.

During the time of Amanda's care and after her death, my wife and I had disagreements that we had never had before. This was normal because we had feelings that we had never experienced before. No marriage course had ever told us how to act while grieving! Things that did not irritate me before now irritated me. Things that were funny before were no longer funny. Things that were important before were no longer important. The same was true of my wife. Grief had transformed us into two different people!

Some time after Amanda died, someone told me that over fifty percent of the couples who have an infant die separate within two years of their child's death. I do not know the accuracy of these numbers, but I do know that many marriages fall apart after a tragedy during the grieving process. I have dealt with couples who unfortunately are now separated after their child's sickness, their child's death, or some other loss in their life. At this point, we need to understand that it happens. How sad for one tragedy to lead to another. We must understand that grief has this power.

B.   GRIEF CAN ALSO WEAKEN THE
       PARENT/CHILD RELATIONSHIP.

This happens for several reasons. Some children grow away from a parent because of feelings of guilt, resentment, and other feelings that are associated with grief. I know of one instance where a mother died and the son's relationship with his father fell apart because he felt that his father should have cared for his mother differently. Others have felt like a parent should have been there more during their tragedy.

The parent/child relationship can also be weakened because of the parent's reaction to his child's grief. I have talked to parents who avoided their child when he needed them most because they could not handle being around their child while he was grieving. Other parents have seen their relationship with their child hurt because they felt guilty for not being able to protect him from his loss.

Likewise, a parent can lose a spouse and feel like his children could have done more while he was grieving. This many times is true. Feelings of abandonment often accompany grief in a situation like this.

C.   MANY TIMES GRIEF WEAKENS THE
       SIBLING RELATIONSHIP.

This happens for many of the same reasons as in the parent/child relationship. (Refer to the previous paragraph.)

D. IT IS SOMEWHAT COMMON FOR GRIEF TO WEAKEN SOME FRIEND RELATIONSHIPS.

This is particularly true in the situation of a death. It is common because many times the common bond of the relationship was the loved one who died. Now that your loved one is gone, your paths do not cross, nor do you have anything in common. You have lost someone that you love and so has this friend. It is to be expected for this particular relationship to weaken.

E. GRIEF CAN WEAKEN THE PASTOR/ CHURCH MEMBER RELATIONSHIP.

Logic tells us that you must first have a pastor before you can have a relationship with him. Likewise, you must first have a relationship with your pastor before it can be weakened.

Speaking to those with a pastor, you should understand that grief can weaken your relationship with him. From my experience in dealing with people who are grieving, I would say the only way to weaken your relationship with your pastor is not to involve your pastor in your recovery process. He may bring an encouraging message during the Sunday Morning service; but if you are not there to hear it, the message is not going to do you any good. You should seek his counsel and prayers during your time of grief. As you know, grief turns your world upside down; and it is important that you have someone to give you direction in your life.

III.   GRIEF WILL CULTIVATE NEW RELATIONSHIPS.

During the grieving process you will meet many people that you normally would not meet. Let me give you a few examples. During my daughter's hospital stay, we met many doctors and nurses. Many of whom we still keep in touch with now. I would have rather my daughter never been sick and never have to spend a day in the hospital. Obviously, everyone who is experiencing loss would rather have his loved one back than to meet a million new people. However, we can not change what has happened; and if we look hard enough, we will see new relationships form during our time of grief.

Sometimes you cross the path of someone, and you connect with him right away. In our case this happened with a lady named Dianne Rigby. Dianne works for Community Hospice Pediatrics Division. Amanda was assigned to Dianne. Immediately, she and my wife formed a bond. Dianne was a great encouragement to my wife during this hard time. Even after Amanda died, we have stayed close to Dianne. We do not see each other all the time or even talk on a regular basis, but there is a friendship that was formed during our time of grief. It is not uncommon for Dianne to call me to see if I can help another family who has lost a child. One Christmas season, Dianne arranged for us to shoot a television commercial for Community Hospice. At the last Amanda Foundation Golf Classic, I recognized

Dianne for her outstanding work with families in their time of grief.

The point I am trying to make is that during our time of grief, God sends the right people across our path. Some wonderful lasting friendships can be made if we are aware of the opportunities that come our way. Many times we miss out on these new relationships because we do not realize that this is possible.

GRIEF TIP
Right now take a look at all your relationships. It is important for you to realize how grief has affected each one of your relationships. Are they stronger? Are they weaker? Are they stronger in some areas and weaker in other areas?

SECTION THREE — RECOVERY

12

Obstacles You Face on the Road to Recovery

As you know, recovery is a hard place to get to. Grief can be devastating. Your loss is difficult to deal with. As hard as it is dealing with loss and grief, you can recover. Recovery is a place that you can get to; but in order to get to recovery, there are obstacles that you will face. In this chapter, I will deal with two obstacles specifically.

I.   ACCEPTANCE

When I go to the children's hospital to make visits or give out gift bags, I always get asked this question by someone. "How do you do this?" Some do not even ask the question. These people tell me that it is remarkable that I am able to do this. At first, I did not think anything of it. After I kept getting the same response, I began looking for the answer. How was I able to do this? The reason why I can visit parents of sick children, visit children in the same rooms my daughter was in, and have a desire to help people can be answered with one word–*acceptance*.

Does this mean that my emotions are in complete

control and my mind does not wander? No. There are times when I recall some horrible memories. There have been occasions when I have been overwhelmed by my emotions. I can continue though because I have overcome this obstacle. I have accepted the fact that my daughter was very sick. I have accepted the fact that she has passed away. I have accepted the fact that I will never see her grow up. This does not mean I like the fact that she suffered or endured the things she endured, but I have accepted it. Many people will never recover from their loss because they can not accept their loss. People suffer for a lifetime because they refuse to overcome this obstacle.

The pain from losing my little girl will never go away. I have accepted it as part of my life. What loss has caused you pain? Have you accepted it? I am not saying this is easy. Babies are not supposed to die. Having a child is supposed to be a happy occasion. I have to accept the fact that in this instance my baby did die; and by faith, I accept it as part of God's plan.

Whatever your loss is you must accept it. If you have gone through a divorce, you must accept the fact that you are now single. If you have lost your health, you must accept the fact that you are sick. Acceptance is the key that opens the door to recovery. If you are standing at the door of recovery, quit knocking to get in. Take the key and open the door yourself. Acceptance does not take the pain away but does offer some relief on the journey through heartache.

II.   UNDERSTANDING THERE IS GOOD IN EVERY SITUATION.

Whenever I am asked how I am able to get through the pain associated with losing a child, I explain that I have accepted this as part of my life. The next obstacle is understanding that there is good in every situation. I have been asked how can anything good come from a child dying. How can anything good come from my husband or wife leaving me? It all depends on how you look at your situation. I am not saying that loss is good. I have a saying that I try to live by. "Life could be better, but it could also be worse."

How could anything good come from a baby dying? I can answer that question. Amanda is not suffering anymore. Amanda experienced much pain and suffering her entire life. I hated to watch her suffer. There is nothing more devastating than watching your child suffer and not being able to offer relief. Amanda will never have another seizure or be poked by another needle. The fact that my daughter will never suffer again is good. During the course of one conversation with Shelly Grabow, (The family in Chapter 3) she told me that she was thankful for the time she did have with her sons before they died. That is finding good in a bad situation.

You must discover what is good in your situation. More important than actually finding the good is looking for it. The reason this is such a big obstacle is that most people when they experience loss get a fatalistic attitude. Because something horrible has happened, you understand that you are vulnerable to the most painful things. Your mind-set becomes one that believes the bad is always going to happen. When you tell yourself that there is good in every situation, you begin looking for it as opposed to waiting for the bad to happen.

My wife's parents separated when she was very young. She grew up without a father. Of course, this was not an ideal situation. My wife, along with her mother and brother had to move from Louisiana to California. My wife's family struggled financially. She faced the many insecurities and struggles that a child faces in a divorce, yet there was good in this situation. Because her parents separated, she was forced to move. Because she was forced to move, she heard of a college that she would never have heard of. She went to that college and met me. We were married and now have a wonderful life together. We met because of a bad situation. I am not advocating that divorce equals wonderfully happy success stories. I am advocating, however, that you can find good in every situation.

If acceptance is the key to opening the door to recovery, then understanding that there is good in every situation is what gives us the boldness to walk through it. The two work together. My wife accepted the fact that her parents divorced. She did not blame her mom, God, or anyone else. Her acceptance gave her the opportunity to find good in her situation. The acceptance of your loss will enable you to look for the good in your own situation.

13

Three Questions to Ask When You Experience Loss

When we face loss in our lives, it is a normal thing to ask questions. Many of these questions offer no benefit to us. There are three questions we should ask that will be beneficial to us if we take the time to answer them.

I.   WHAT AM I SUPPOSED TO LEARN?

Through my journey of heartache, I believe there have been lessons I was and am supposed to learn. I believe loss is a teacher. Loss has lessons it will teach us if we are willing to learn them.

It is sad when a child sits in the class of a knowledgeable teacher and refuses to learn or apply himself. This is what a lot of people do when they experience loss. They refuse to learn any lessons from life. Rightfully so we would encourage and even prod the child to learn from his teacher. The average person with heartache needs to be prodded to learn as well. A common reason that a child is not motivated to learn from a teacher is that the teacher is firm or requires a lot from him. What the child does not understand is that is the kind of teacher who teaches him the most. Loss is likewise a firm teacher and requires a lot from us. We can learn some valuable lessons from this hard teacher.

Personally, I learned many things from my loss. One lesson that I learned is to never take one day with my family for granted. My family has benefitted from this lesson. I believe I am more thoughtful and sensitive to their needs. I enjoy each moment with my loved ones even more now.

I learned so many valuable lessons from my loss. I learned them because I asked this question. What am I supposed to learn? If you ask the question, you will be amazed at what the answers might be.

GRIEF TIP
Mark a place in a journal or notebook for you to list the lessons you have learned.

II. HOW SHOULD I CHANGE?

It was very evident to me during my time of heartache that there were things that I needed to change. Some of these things were obvious; some were not so obvious. Some things that needed changing were made evident for the first time.

Since my daughter's death, many people have told me that I have changed. I must point out that some changes will happen naturally because of your loss. Other changes only take place if you determine to make them. If I could personally sit down with you, perhaps I could point out some changes that you should make.

During your time of grief, you probably would not be receptive to them. This is why you must ask this question of yourself.

Most people will make the mistake of trying to change things that they can not change. You can not go back in time and change what has happened. You can not change the way someone feels. You only have the power to change yourself. What should you change in your life today? Whatever it is, use your loss to better yourself.

GRIEF TIP
Make a list of changes that you can make in your life. Use this list to empower you to recover.

III. WHO AM I SUPPOSED TO HELP?

This is the hard question to get people to ask. I am the one hurting. I am the one who was left behind. I was the one emotionally scarred. I need help.

Yes, if you have lost a loved one, you need help. If you are the one with loss, you need help. Nevertheless, there is someone that you can help.

I have been amazed at the number of people I have been able to help since Amanda died. The great reason that I have been able to help others is the fact that I have been willing to help others. I asked myself the question, "Who am I supposed to help?"

I have discovered something wonderful through all of the help I have given. When I help others, I do not hurt as badly. When I get involved in what they need, I do not focus on my loss. Helping others will help you.

How do you help yourself? Help someone else.

GRIEF TIP
Make a list of who it is in your life that you are supposed to help or could help.

None of us like questions in our life. Without questions there would be no answers. The best way to find the answer is with a question. When you have answers to the three questions in this chapter, it is a good sign that you are on your way to recovery.

14

Closure

Everything looked great. It was not every day that you see one of our church buildings decorated as a casino. The ladies at the party store told my wife and me that they had never sold casino decorations to a church before. Slot machines, cards, and poker chips were just a few of the things that were plastered on the walls of the gymnasium. The eight-foot stack of dice was my personal favorite. The word *bet* was used in different phrases that were used with the wall decorations. You are probably wondering what kind of church function has anything to do with a casino. This particular church function was for one of my brothers. No, he was not a recovering gambler. This was a reception so that our church people could say good-bye. He had been working on our church staff for years, but now felt that God was moving him to Las Vegas to pastor a new church.

Of course, when this was announced to our church, many people were saddened by the news because they did not want to see him go. Our church people understood the importance of following the direction that God leads but were sorry to see that direction taking him away. This reception gave people a chance to properly say good-bye and to tell he and his wife how much the two of them meant. Mark had been serving as our youth pastor. He was a big part of the young people's lives. He had helped many of them with problems and heartaches. He had taken them on youth trips and many different activities. He had led them to make many of their spiritual decisions. His leaving for Las Vegas was going to create a void in their lives. This reception provided a way for these young people to say good-bye.

The young people would have a new youth pastor. The new youth pastor would love them and try just as hard to help them. In order for these teenagers to start accepting their new youth pastor, they had to have an opportunity to properly say good-bye to their previous youth pastor. They had to have closure to a previous part of their life. Did this mean that they would forget my brother, Mark? Did this mean they would stop loving him? Did this mean that they would try to replace him? The answer to all of these questions is no. However, they needed to say good-bye.

Whenever you experience loss, it is necessary to the recovery process to say good-bye. You must say good-bye to loved ones, dreams, or missed opportunities. Many people are struggling with grief because of their inability to say good-bye. There were two different times that I said good-bye to my daughter. The first time was the morning that Amanda passed away. My wife and I had rushed to the hospital after Heather's mom had called to say Amanda was not doing well. The following is an except from Chapter 22 of *An Angel Among Us*.

When we got to Amanda's bedside, we could see that it would not be long before she went to Heaven. Heather rubbed Amanda's head while I held Amanda's hand. By this time, we could no longer hold back the tears. Through tears and sobs, Heather told Amanda that it was okay for her to go. Neither one of us wanted her to suffer anymore. We had always told each other that we would know when it was time for Amanda to go. There was no doubt that this was her time.

The nurse then asked if Heather wanted to hold her. Heather said she did, so the nurse turned off her monitors, and put Amanda in Heather's lap. As I knelt beside Heather, we both told Amanda how much we loved her. We also told her that we would miss her, but that we were glad that very soon she would not suffer anymore.

I do not believe that my wife and I fully understood the importance of what we did that day. Although it was a hard thing to do, we told Amanda good-bye. The second time that I told Amanda good-bye was over a period of several days. After Amanda's funeral, I went to her grave alone. I spent time there alone. I wept, but I also told Amanda good-bye. If I had not done this, I do not believe I would have been able to face the struggle with recovery that lay ahead.

There are many reasons why people do not seek closure in their life by saying good-bye. Some do not realize the importance. Others have given up hope. From my experience and study of grief, I believe there are four factors that play a part in failures to say good-bye. The following are excuses that we use in justifying our failure for closure through a good-bye.

1.   SAYING GOOD-BYE MEANS I AM TRYING TO FORGET.

This is not at all true. Although there are some aspects of every loss we would like to forget, saying good-bye does not mean we are trying to forget a loved one. Saying good-bye is acknowledging that we have lost someone or something that we cared about.

> Saying good-bye is acknowledging that we have lost someone or something that we cared about.

When my brother moved to Las Vegas, I said good-bye. I have not forgotten him. There are times when I am reminded of him. When I said good-bye, I was acknowledging that I would not see him often or spend time with him like before he moved.

2.   TO SAY GOOD-BYE IS TO SAY THAT I DO NOT LOVE WHAT I LOST ANYMORE.

I love my daughters, Alyssa and Anna. I love my daughter, Amanda. The fact that Amanda is not here does not change the fact that I love her. Because I told her good-bye does not mean I love her any less than her sisters. I love all my children. I just have to go through life without one of them.

We hurt because we have lost something that we love. When we say good-bye, we are heading down the path of recovery. The pain does not go away,

> When we say good-bye, we are heading down the path of recovery.

but it is eased somewhat because we are starting to recover. We associate less love with less pain. This is not true. This is an important lesson to understand. Because I am bringing some closure does not mean I do no longer love.

3.   SAYING GOOD-BYE MEANS I HAVE TO ACCEPT CIRCUMSTANCES THAT I CAN NOT CHANGE.

Saying good-bye is facing reality. I had to accept that I had no say in my daughter's fate. I was powerless to help her in any way. When I took those trips to the cemetery to visit her grave, I was facing reality. I had to be honest with myself. I had to accept the fact that all of my dreams for Amanda would never come to fruition. I would never see her walk. I would never see her play. I would never see her again. By saying good-bye, I was deciding not to live in a fantasy land but accept the horrible, bitter slap of reality.

> By saying good-bye, I was deciding not to live in a fantasy land but accept the horrible, bitter slap of reality.

A divorcee can not change the fact that he or she is divorced. To say good-bye to a relationship is to accept this as fact. An abandoned child can not make a parent love him. To say good-bye is to accept the reality of his loneliness. To say good-bye to a loved one is to accept the fact that someone you loved is gone. Saying good-bye makes us overcome the obstacle of facing reality.

Accepting our loss is not fun. It is quite painful, but it is necessary to be able to say good-bye.

Even when we remove these common excuses, saying good-bye is a hard thing to do. Good-byes are not fun, nor are they easy. In my experience, I have found that there are three factors that make it difficult for those grieving to seek closure.

1.   WE NEVER WANTED TO LOSE WHAT WE LOST.

The brokenhearted divorcee never wanted his or her marriage to fall apart. The grieving parent never wanted to lose a child. The lonely widow never wanted to face a day without her lifelong partner. We have a hard time saying good-bye because we are forced to deal with circumstances we never expected or asked for.

One of life's cruelest characteristics is to give us loss that we did not ask for and do not have the ability to do anything about. I often visit the local children's hospital. On this particular occasion, I was visiting a family who had a child in the pediatric Intensive Care Unit. After I left their child's room, I thought about how unfair life can be. This family did not want their child to be sick. As I walked down the hall to the exit, I was struck with a thought that I have during every visit. As I passed the rooms on the way to the exit, I thought of the fact that many of these kids will never go home. Their parents never asked for this situation. The husband or wife did not ask for the divorce papers he or she was issued. We do not ask for our evening to be interrupted with a phone call telling us that a loved one has passed away. A patient never asks for the disease that the doctor tells him he has. We have a hard time saying good-bye because our mind reminds us that we are dealing with something that we never wanted and never asked for.

2.   WHEN WE SAY GOOD-BYE, WE MUST ACKNOWLEDGE OUR HEARTACHE AND LOSS.

We must look our grief in the face. We are forced to once again remind ourselves of our loss. When I said good-bye to Amanda, I had to acknowledge that she was gone. I could not put my loss in the back of my mind. I could not pretend that this tragedy never happened. When I said good-bye, I acknowledged the fact that my daughter was not going to be with me anymore.

3.   WHEN WE SAY GOOD-BYE, WE MUST FACE PAST FAILURES.

Earlier in this chapter, I mentioned that I had spent time at my daughter's grave saying good-bye. My biggest struggle through the whole process of saying good-bye was facing my failures. I spent a lot of time at Amanda's grave telling her that I was sorry. I could not help but feel that for some reason everything that had happened was my fault.

While I was there, so many things came to mind. I remember times when I could have held her, and I did not. I remember getting frustrated because I would be so tired and have to get up to care for her. All these failures flooded my mind.

> I could not say good-bye until I faced myself and my past failures.

As her father, I should have been able to prevent this from happening. At least that is what I thought.

I could not say good-bye until I faced myself and my past failures. Many struggle with this whole process. I should have done this differently, or I should have done that differently. Saying good-bye is hard because we must accept our failures. This would include sorting through the past and honestly evaluating where we failed. Even though we think we have failed in many areas, we actually did not fail; but we can not determine that fact until we approach the past with the attitude of being willing to forgive our failures. In order to achieve closure, we must look our failures in the face and accept them.

Saying good-bye is a transitional phase in life. By achieving closure, I am moving from grief to recovery. If we want to successfully move from one phase of grief to the next, we must loosen our grip on the past. Saying good-bye means we are accepting the fact that our life is not going to include whatever it is that we lost. It does not matter if you lost a loved one, a dream, a job, or health. You are allowing yourself to be honest with your present situation. This realization will transition you to be able to begin to recover.

> Saying good-bye is a transitional phase in life.

THE NECESSITY OF A MEANS TO SAY GOOD-BYE

Hopefully, by this point of the chapter, you realize the importance of saying good-bye. You might be asking yourself the question, "How do I say good-bye?" The generalized answer to that question is that you must find a way to say good-bye. Let me explain.

Each person must say good-bye in his own way. I already told you my way of saying good-bye. Consider these different ways of saying good-bye.

- Funeral
- Graveside
- Writing
- Visit to childhood home
- Clean out loved one's possessions
- Sell home after death or divorce
- Change professions
- Pick up a hobby

You might find one of these is the same as your means of closure. The important thing is that you find the means to say good-bye.

15

Allow Your Loss to Motivate You

It is sad to think of how many lives have been derailed by tragedy. As we have already discussed, grief can paralyze you in so many ways. We must take action to overcome grief.

This is not a hard concept to understand. However, finding a way to motivate yourself to action is a different story. We can all think of things that might make the grief process a little easier, but can we find enough strength and desire to do these things?

I believe this chapter is crucial to recovery. We must find something to motivate us when we grieve. We have already discussed that grief takes many things from you including a desire to do things that must be done. We find that the things that motivated us before no longer motivate us. The drive to succeed or excel no longer exists as it once did. The fact of the matter is this; we must find motivation from somewhere. We must find some way to make ourselves do all the things that we need to do. We need to find a way to make ourselves accomplish the things we could accomplish in spite of our grief.

Allow me to share with you the answer to these

questions. Allow your loss to motivate you. This may be confusing to you. It is your loss that is causing you to grieve, but it is your loss that can motivate you to overcome grief. Whenever I counsel with someone who is grieving, this is the advice that I always give them. Many times this is confusing until I explain exactly what I mean. Allow me to illustrate this point by using my personal experiences.

> It is your loss that is causing you to grieve, but it is your loss that can motivate you to overcome grief.

MAKE YOUR LOVED ONE PROUD.

Parents want their children to be proud of them. I want my two daughters, Alyssa and Anna, to be proud of who their father is. Likewise, I want Amanda to be proud of me as well.

In the Bible, Hebrews 12:1 tells us, "Wherefore seeing we also are compassed about with so great a cloud of witnesses, let us lay aside every weight, and the sin which doth so easily beset us, and let us run with patience the race that is set before us." I know that my daughter is part of that "great cloud of witnesses." As she watches her father run his race, I want her to be proud of me.

There have been times when I have not wanted to do the things I knew I had to do. Grief has even caused me to question my life's direction and my own life's meaning. My motivation on these days is simply this: I want Amanda to be proud that Greg Neal is her

> I want my daughter, as part of this "great cloud of witnesses," to see her father overcoming obstacles in his life.

father. I had one person tell me that our life now does not affect our loved ones who have passed away. I do not think that way. I want my daughter, as part of this "great cloud of witnesses," to see her father overcoming obstacles in his life. Every time I help someone else with his problems, I picture my daughter pointing me out to the other witnesses and exclaiming, "That's my dad!". I want her to be able to brag to the other witnesses about how good I am to her mother. As I rear and provide for her sisters, I want her to proclaim that I am the world's greatest dad. This way of thinking has transformed my life.

I challenge you to motivate yourself this way. Discipline your thinking in this way. Many times the first question asked of me by those who are grieving is "How do you make yourself get out of bed and face the day?". My answer is that my daughter's death will not be the reason that I failed, but rather the reason that I succeeded. Making my daughter proud is my motivation.

> My daughter's death will not be the reason that I failed, but rather the reason that I succeeded.

What are you grieving the loss of? Perhaps it was not the death of a child but of a parent, grandparent, sibling, or a close friend. Make your motivation the fact that you want to make that loved one proud. You do not make them proud by the way you try to disassociate from grief, but instead by the way you go on in spite of it.

GRIEF TIP
Determine that your loss will not be the excuse you use as to why you failed, but will be the reason you succeeded.

BUILD A LEGACY FOR YOUR LOVED ONE.

After Amanda passed, away I had to accept many different facts. One fact that was especially hard to deal with was the realization that some people would never know her. As time passed, people would forget about Amanda. People we met in the future would not even know that we had another daughter. I believe it is important to every one who has lost a loved one that his loved one be remembered. However, it is a natural thing for other people to forget.

I want people to remember my daughter. I knew for that to happen, I must do something so she would be remembered. I decided to build a legacy for Amanda. If Amanda is to be remembered, it will be because I did something to make her be remembered. The following are a couple of ways that I have built a legacy for Amanda.

THE AMANDA FOUNDATION

The Amanda Foundation is a charity (501c) that I began with the purpose of helping families who find themselves in a similar situation that my family found ourselves in. The purpose of this foundation is to support and financially aid families who have a child who is terminally ill or have a child in a life-threatening situation. We supply funds for various needs such as nurse care and doctor's bills. We also provide support for families who have a child pass away, and we help with funeral expenses as well. We also provide vacations so families can get away after experiencing such a great loss.

This experience has been incredible. Although it has been difficult and time consuming to get a new charity going, it has been very rewarding. We have been able to encourage and help many people. We have been able to issue grants to help pay for medical bills. Every Christmas, I and my volunteers go room to room at the local children's hospital. We drop off gift bags of snacks and gifts such as stuffed animals. I will never forget the looks on the faces of so many of these kids. The parents told me over and over how grateful they were that I cared enough to come by. I could tell them that I understood what they were dealing with and that I was glad to help. By leaving printed information and the book I wrote about Amanda, I was able to tell about the little girl who was the inspiration behind the foundation. Recently, I was able to send a couple on a vacation who had lost their infant daughter. I enjoyed sending them as much as they enjoyed going. The local news filmed as I went to their house and told them that they would be going on a vacation. You would have thought I had just told them they had won a million dollars. This experience was very rewarding. This couple understood that this was happening because of my little girl.

I host a fund-raising golf tournament every year. It is very exciting to get local businesses to support this event as well as to see the number of golfers who play in the tournament. After the round of golf, we have our annual celebration banquet. During this time, I hand out the golf awards as well as make special presentations. It is during this time that I distribute grants to qualifying families as well as recognize "difference makers" in the community. I explain that this day is the fulfillment of a dream. I also explain that on this day my daughter, Amanda lives. She lives through me and those who make it possible to help these other families. To those that I am able to help through The Amanda Foundation my daughter might as well be a super hero. It is the legacy that is hers that came through when the helpless needed help.

Since I started The Amanda Foundation, the local news has done a story on Amanda twice. I have had a story printed in the local newspaper about Amanda. Local businesses have "adopted" the foundation as their charity. We have established a successful annual fund-raising golf tournament, as well as helped many families financially and emotionally deal with the loss of a child. It is not uncommon for someone to come up to me in public and comment on the good that I am doing because he recognized me from the local television news or the newspaper. When I take all this into consideration, it gives me great joy and satisfaction because of the legacy that is being built for Amanda.

AMANDA'S PANDAS

When Amanda was alive, we often referred to her as "Amanda Panda." This was our nickname for her. After her death, we collected panda bears. The sight of a panda bear brings back many memories of Amanda for us.

One of my duties as an Assistant Pastor is overseeing the church nurseries. Recently, I was giving much thought to restructuring and reorganizing our nursery ministry. I approached my father, who is the Pastor, with the idea of dedicating the nurseries to the memory of Amanda. He told me that he had also thought of the very same thing. I gave this idea more thought, and the Amanda's Pandas nursery ministry was started.

The idea of this ministry is simple. If Amanda were able to be in our church nurseries, I would want her to get the best care possible. I believe the nursery workers would do their very best to offer her the best care available. That is the level of care we strive to give in our nurseries. Because each child is special, every child in our nurseries is an "Amanda's Panda." There are panda bears painted on the walls. Each child has an "Amanda's Pandas" name tag placed on his diaper bag. These children are not like other children. They are part of a very special group. They are "Amanda's Pandas."

It gives me great satisfaction every time I walk down the hall leading to the nurseries in our church building. Upon entering the nursery suites, you pass a picture of Amanda. Likewise, every parent that brings his child to those nurseries does so while building Amanda's legacy.

I decided after Amanda died that I wanted people to know who she was ten years from now. I decided to build her a legacy. Because of this, her short life will be making a difference for years to come.

GRIEF TIP
Determine how you can build a legacy for your loved one.

TURN YOUR TRAGEDY INTO YOUR LIFE'S MISSION.

I believe you can use your tragedy to motivate you by turning your tragedy into your life's mission. I discovered during Amanda's hospital stays that there were great numbers of people who faced the same prospect of tragedy with their child that I faced. I now realize how many parents lose a child every day. I can understand the feelings that they are going through. I know the valleys that lay ahead for them. These are reasons why I want to help as many of these parents as possible. I have decided to make it my life's mission to help as many families as possible who have lost a child.

16

The Legacy of Saniah Harrigan

In the previous chapter, I wrote several ways for us to allow our tragedy to motivate us. One of these ways is to build a legacy for our loved one. In this chapter, I want to give you an illustration of building a legacy. I want to tell you of Wilvern and Omega, and the legacy that they are building for their daughter Saniah. In order to do so, I must tell you Saniah's story.

Saniah Harrigan was born on June 16, 2003. Saniah was born premature at 36 weeks. Because of her premature birth, it was necessary to place her on a ventilator so she could breathe properly. Fortunately she had to be on the ventilator for only one day. After she was taken off of the ventilator, it was still necessary for her to be on oxygen. Wilvern and Omega knew that this was fairly standard for premature babies. They were hopeful that Saniah's hospital stay would just be for a few weeks.

Unfortunately the desired short stay became an undesired longer stay of two and a half months. During Saniah's prolonged stay, some serious problems were discovered. Saniah had an undersized cerebellum, which controls the muscular movements of the body. Her corpus callosum was missing which prevented her cerebral hemispheres from communicating. Saniah had to have her first surgery during this stay. It was discovered that her intestines did not grow correctly. Surgery was performed to correct this problem, and Saniah recovered well. Saniah was not eating very well which resulted in minimal weight gain. She had to have a gastrointestinal tube surgically placed into her stomach. This tube would allow her to get the proper amount of food. Saniah had to have splints on her hands because she was having trouble keeping them open. In addition to the splints, she began having physical therapy five days a week. In spite of these problems, Saniah showed improvement and was discharged.

Wilvern and Omega were thrilled to finally have their daughter home. Only three weeks had passed when Saniah had a setback. She stopped breathing while at day care. She was rushed to the hospital where she was admitted for observation and tests. It was concluded that Saniah had acid reflux. She was given medication and discharged.

Being home again was refreshing for Wilvern and Omega, but the stay at home was cut short when Saniah was diagnosed with pneumonia five days later. An anticipated short stay once again turned into a long stay when Saniah began vomiting on a regular basis. It was determined that surgery was necessary to prevent Saniah from continually vomiting her food. While preparing for surgery, the doctors were unable to properly insert a breathing tube. Saniah's airway was "floppy," so it was determined that she needed a tracheotomy.

Saniah successfully made it through surgery and began to recover.

Even though Saniah was having trouble coming off of the ventilator, she eventually was discharged and would be on a home ventilator. Wilvern and Omega enjoyed having Saniah home once again. A couple of months passed without Saniah having to return to the hospital. Unfortunately, during this stay at home Saniah's little body finally gave out. After a struggle with life, Saniah passed away leaving behind a heartbroken mom and dad.

I met Wilvern and Omega at my annual hospital event during the Christmas season. They came through the line of the free barbecue dinner that I have for parents and medical staff. They captured my attention, so I followed them and sat down with them while they ate. I explained to them what The Amanda Foundation does, and they told me about their daughter, Saniah. I told them that I would like to help them whenever I was able.

I called them after several months. The timing was perfect because I was unaware that Saniah had passed away the previous week. I went to see them and offer my help in any way. I offered some counsel on what they would face since I had experienced losing a child as well. I also told them that I wanted to do something for them, as money would allow.

A short time later, I called Wilvern and Omega and told them the local news wanted to interview them. The news wanted them to tell how my foundation had helped this couple. What they did not know is that we had a surprise for them. When I knocked on the door, the camera was already rolling. We walked into the house, and I told them that The Amanda Foundation was sending them on an all-expense paid trip. They were surprised and very happy about this.

After their trip, they told me how much it meant to them that I had been there for them. They conveyed to me that Amanda's life had made a difference because they had been helped. They also told me that they wanted to help in the future with the foundation. I wished them well and told them to call me if they ever needed me.

Unexpectedly, I received a phone call from Omega asking me to meet them one afternoon. We set the time and the place to meet. When we sat down to talk, they handed me a card. Wilvern explained that they were so grateful for my helping them when they needed it. I opened the card and realized that there was a check enclosed. When I saw the amount of the check, I was speechless. I was holding in my hand a donation for the foundation that was the single largest gift I had ever received. Wilvern and Omega explained to me that they were making this donation in Saniah's memory. It was their desire to make her short life count as I had done with Amanda. This was overwhelming for me because this was a fulfillment of a goal of mine. Here was someone I had helped through their tragedy now helping others.

Here is Saniah's legacy. That money was used to help other families who had lost a child. It was also used to fund gift bags for all of the children at the children's hospital. It also funded a "Nurses Appreciation Day" that The Amanda Foundation sponsored at the same hospital. This all took place because Wilvern and Omega decided to build a legacy for their daughter.

Hopefully, this example will inspire someone to build a legacy for his loved one. If your loss was not death, you can still make a difference in someone else's situation. They knew that they were making a difference, and they were deciding to overcome. Saniah would be so proud. My advice to all who have experienced loss is this. Follow their example.

17

Carrie Moon:
An Example for Caregivers

Through all of my dealings with different people and different experiences, I have had many caregivers ask me to offer what I could on helping others with their grief. It is because of this fact that I decided to write a chapter giving some advice to caregivers. I have never been a doctor or nurse, but believe I am in a unique position to offer some helpful thought to doctors or nurses.

When I decided to write this chapter, I was sure of two things. The first thing that I was sure of was the fact that this information could help all caregivers. Usually, when I use the word *caregiver,* I am talking about doctors and nurses of all kinds and those who have the difficult time caring for a loved one who can not care for himself. This chapter might be informative for all caregivers, but it is specifically written for those who are in the medical profession in some capacity. The second thing that I was certain of is the belief that the best way to help relate these helpful tips would be to do so by giving an example of the proper way to do things from someone who is a caregiver. In order to accomplish this, I chose someone who dealt with my wife and I personally at some point in my daughter's life. This person actually dealt with us the day of Amanda's death. In Chapter 2, "Grief Defined," you read an excerpt of Chapter 22 of *An Angel Among Us*. I feel in order to make the necessary points in this chapter I need to print a portion of this same excerpt. I believe doing so will be beneficial to you. I present to you Carrie Moon: an example for caregivers.

We took the elevator to the third floor. We rushed into the Intensive Care Unit. I'll never forget the looks on the faces of the doctors and nurses as they watched us hurry to Amanda's room. Each face seemed to say, "I'm sorry." When we went into Amanda's room, Heather's mom and brother were there, along with a hospital chaplain. When we got to Amanda's bedside, we could see that it would not be long before she went to Heaven. Heather rubbed Amanda's head while I held her hand. By this time we could no longer hold back the tears. Through tears and sobs, Heather told Amanda that it was okay for her to go. Neither one of us wanted her to suffer any more. We had always told each other that we would know when it was time for Amanda to go. There was no doubt that this was her time.

After a few minutes, one of Amanda's nurses came in and told us that when Amanda's heart rate dropped she had to bag her with the ambu bag to bring her heart rate and oxygen level back up. We told her that we did not want this because it was time for her to go to Heaven. Some might wonder how we could do this, but it was not a difficult thing to do. We had watched her suffer so much, and we did not want this to be prolonged. We knew that God had decided that this was the time that

He would take her to be with Him.

The nurse then asked if Heather wanted to hold her. Heather said she did, so the nurse turned her monitors off, and put Amanda in Heather's lap. As I knelt beside Heather, we both told Amanda how much we loved her. We also told her that we would miss her, but that we were glad that very soon she would not suffer any more.

The nurse mentioned in this excerpt does have a name. Her name is Carrie Moon. I do not ever remember meeting Carrie before the day of Amanda's death. However, I have not forgotten her since that day. If she had been one of Amanda's nurses prior to this day, I do not recall. I did not even know her name at the printing of *An Angel Among Us*. I have since talked to her many times and consider her a friend. Whether you are a caregiver or someone who is grieving, you may be asking yourself this question, "How does a nurse become friends with the parent of a patient who dies in her care?" I believe my charity work at the hospital has something to do with it, but I also believe Carrie's actions were exemplary and the comfort she presented is seared in my memory.

I am sure that there is training on how to deal with people who are in the situation that I was in that day. I do not claim to be an expert in the training of caregivers. However, I probably could be called an expert on how I felt that day and what I needed to hear and know. There were five things that Carrie did that made this hard time easier for my wife and me.

1.   CARRIE WAS CONSIDERATE OF OUR PRIVACY.

During our last few minutes with Amanda, my wife and I wanted to be alone. We were completely focused on these last moments with our daughter. Whenever Carrie did come into the room she was quiet and non-intrusive. She said only what was necessary to us. When she did ask us a question, she did not hover over us waiting for an answer. We were able to spend the last moments of our daughter's life with her in privacy.

2.   CARRIE TALKED TO US NOT AT US.

As one might imagine, that day Amanda passed away was a very difficult day. It was difficult because of Amanda's death, but it was also difficult because of the different emotions and decisions that we faced. One thing that made this bearable was the fact that Carrie "talked us through it." We had to decide how long to prolong Amanda's life and how much time we wanted to spend with her and who we allowed to see her. Whenever Carrie spoke to us, I never felt like she was talking at us. By doing so, she put us at ease. Any pressure put on us at this time would have been devastating. The fact that we felt like Carrie was talking to us had a calming affect on us.

3.   CARRIE MADE US BELIEVE THAT SHE CARED.

I do not know how many patients Carrie had that day, but I felt like Amanda was her only one. She never seemed distracted by anything. I felt like we had her complete attention. She told us that she was very sorry for our loss. I am sure that is what every nurse says to the family who has lost a loved one. It was not the words that made me feel she was sorry; it was the fact that I could look into her eyes and see that she was sorry. There were a couple of other things that she did that made me think she cared, but it was what I saw in her eyes that made me believe that she did.

4.   CARRIE GAVE US ASSURANCE.

During Amanda's last few moments, we were faced with a decision. Did we want her life prolonged? It was inevitable that Amanda's life would end soon. Should we prolong it so we could spend more time with her. We decided that we would let Amanda go peacefully because we felt that it was God's time. Afterwards, my wife and I were standing outside the waiting room when Carrie brought us a few of Amanda's things. It was at this time Carrie assured us that we had done the right thing. I felt like we did, but it was very comforting to hear her tell us that we did. Even to this day, I am comforted by the fact that we were assured we did what was best for our daughter.

5.   CARRIE ASKED US WHAT WE WANTED
      INSTEAD OF TELLING US WHAT WE SHOULD
      DO.

After Amanda passed away, there were several things Carrie had to ask us about. Some of these questions were: "Did we want anyone else to see Amanda?" "Did we want to donate her organs?" "Did we need counseling?" After each question she asked us what we wanted. She did not ask the question, and then follow it with what she thought. If we asked her for an opinion, she gave it; but only if we asked.

These five things I mentioned may be hospital policy. If so, Carrie fulfilled what the hospital expects of their nurses. However, I have to believe that Carrie went above what was required of her. You can tell someone that you are sorry and not be sincere, but you can not fabricate the concern that shows in the eyes.

Carrie did a great job that day. I wish I had never had to meet her under those conditions. However, she was one of those people who made a difference in a difficult situation, and that is what caregivers do. They make a difference.

18

Where Do I Start?

Where do I start? I believe we all have asked that question. Usually when we face a large or overwhelming project, the hardest thing to do is get started. I have faced many seemingly impossible tasks that weren't so difficult to finish once I finally started the project. I am sure that we have all been in this position staring an impossible task in the face while contemplating where to start. Many times this leaves us frustrated with the feeling of failure. Sometimes we do not get started because we do not know where to start. If we only had instructions for everything that we would ever face, surely we would fail less often.

On August 14, 2001, my daughter, Amanda passed away. This tragic event would force me to deal with many unpleasant and undesired things. After Amanda died, I felt completely overwhelmed. I was overwhelmed by my emotions as well as this mountain of uncertainty in facing the future. Perhaps you can identify with the scene I am describing. If you have lost a loved one, then surely you know the scenario that I am describing. If you have experienced another form of loss, you are certainly aware of this lost feeling also.

After Amanda died, I knew I was supposed to do something; but what was I supposed to do right now? I knew it was important to handle things the right way, but what was the right way? How do I fill this void in my life? A better question was "Could I fill the void in my life?" Where do I start? This emptiness was real and hurt unlike any pain I had ever felt before. Where do I start to fill this void? Where do I start to make the pain go away?

Hopefully this book has given you a place to start. The same place we all start in the journey through heartache—loss. I believe this book has provided some very valuable information that will help you through grief until you find yourself in the place of recovery. Along this journey, you will find some very difficult times. This book was hard to write. It took me back to many painful memories, but I persevered so that I might help you. That is what you must do. Persevere through this painful journey and help someone else along the way. When you are having a particularly hard day, refer to certain chapters or perhaps review the "Grief Tips." Go to www.lossgriefandrecovery.com and make use of this helpful website. You can even sign up to receive a weekly grief tip through e-mail. E-mail me at this website and let me know of your progress.

What do you do now? If I am going to drive from Florida to California, the first thing I must do is get in the car. I must follow directions until I arrive at my destination. If you are to reach your destination of recovery, you must begin your journey from loss through grief.

Waiting for You
by Heather Neal

Saying good-bye is not easy for anyone to do,
Especially when you loved someone
Like I did all of you.

But thank you for understanding
And caring for me so,
Although this is not easy
I was ready to go.

God gave me strength and chose me
For a very special role.
I was able to touch many lives
With my very special soul.

I did my best and fought
For my task to be well done,
And now I am resting
While I watch all of you still run.

Heaven can't be compared to earth
It's such a perfect place;
All the suffering that goes on down there,
Up here there is no trace.

Although I miss you greatly
I'm really doing fine,
And now as I begin to understand
I'm honored to call you mine.

You loved me like no other
You gave me all you had,
You truly are the greatest
Sister, mom, and dad.

Don't forget what I have taught you
About God's love and wondrous grace;
I promise it will all be worth it
When you look into His face.

When your race is over
And your life's work is through
I promise you, my family,
I'll be right here waiting for you.

This beautiful poem was written by Amanda's mother, Heather, after Amanda passed away. Her heartfelt words sum up how she felt after this tragic ordeal. This poem is also an example of the fact that there is much to learn from each experience in life.

Acknowledgments

To complete a book takes the help of many people. This is especially true to complete a book on this subject. Many people were instrumental in the completion of this project.

I am grateful to my wife and children for their encouragement and sacrifice. They sacrificed time with their husband and father, so I could work on this project. They never once complained during the countless hours I spent doing research and writing.

I must thank my father, Tom Neal, for his encouragement to write this book. It was his prodding that finally got me started.

I am grateful to Becky Powell for her tireless effort in layout and design of this book.

Thank you to my high school grammar and composition teacher, Pam Triplett, for her efforts in proofreading. (I guess I was paying attention in class.)

Thank you to my first grief seminar class held at Berean Baptist Church. Your input was instrumental in the development of this book.

Thank you to all those parents who have allowed me to work with you in the loss of your child. I hope I have been at least a small blessing and help to you. Many times you were the inspiration to complete this book.

Thank you to all those who gave your input and testimonials for this book. Your feedback was very encouraging.

I can not write an acknowledgment page without acknowledging God. It was God Who gave me the strength to endure the painful loss of my daughter, and it is God Who has helped me make sense of this tragedy. I hope that I will always please Him, and it is my desire that this book might point others to Him.

The Journey Through Heartache
Notes

The Journey Through Heartache
Notes

The Journey Through Heartache
Notes

The Journey Through Heartache
Notes

_____

_____

_____

_____

_____

_____

_____

_____

_____

_____

_____

_____

_____

_____

_____

_____

_____

_____

_____

_____

_____

_____

The Journey Through Heartache
Notes

_____

_____

_____

_____

_____

_____

_____

_____

_____

_____

_____

_____

_____

_____

_____

_____

_____

_____

_____

_____

_____

_____

The Journey Through Heartache
Notes

_____

_____

_____

_____

_____

_____

_____

_____

_____

_____

_____

_____

_____

_____

_____

_____

_____

_____

_____

_____

_____

The Journey Through Heartache
Notes

_____

_____

_____

_____

_____

_____

_____

_____

_____

_____

_____

_____

_____

_____

_____

_____

_____

_____

_____

_____

_____

_____

_____

The Amanda Foundation

Our Beginning: The Amanda Foundation was started in honor of Amanda Christine Neal who passed away after 8½ months of medical difficulties. Amanda's father, Greg Neal, started the foundation so that through Amanda's memory other families who are experiencing similiar heartache and difficulties could be helped.

Our Purpose: We support and financially aid families who have a child who is terminally ill or have a child with a life-threatening illness. The 24-hour-a-day care that those children require puts a great burden on their families. The Amanda Foundation will provide funds for nurse care and medical supplies when needed. We also provide support for families who have a child pass away, and we will help the family with the funeral expenses. We are concerned with the recovery of those who face tragic events, so we provide a vacation to those families who have experienced such a great loss.

Corporate Sponsorship: The Amanda Foundation's corporate sponsors make a huge difference because of their support. Contact us, so we can set up a unique way for you to make a difference in the lives of those who need our help.

To make a difference contact:
The Amanda Foundation
1530 Business Center Drive, Suite 3
Orange Park, Florida 32003
Phone: 904-269-5422 Fax: 904-264-5290
E-mail: amandafoundation@hotmail.com
Website: 4theamandafoundation.com

All proceeds benefit The Amanda Foundation.
The Amanda Foundation is a non-profit organization
501(c)(3), 509(a)(1) under the National Heritage Foundation.

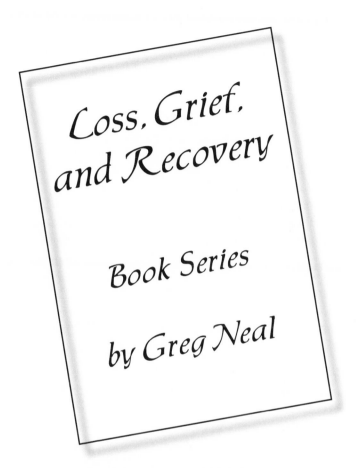

Loss, Grief,
and Recovery

Book Series

by Greg Neal

Look for the next release in this
series of books in the Fall of 2006.

For more information,
please log on to
www.lossgriefandrecovery.com

Read the entire story of the little girl
whose life has touched many.

An Angel Among Us

*"As a registered
nurse, I understand
all too well the mental
turmoil, as well as
how you suffered
through this difficult
experience."*
—Massachusetts

*"The part of the book that
made a great impression
was the list of 10 things you were going to do/
not do as a result of your daughter's medical
difficulties. I copied the list and read it daily."*
—Washington

$12.00 Each

Fill out the order form on the last page of the book or
order online at www.lossgriefandrecovery.com

www.lossgriefandrecovery.com

*Helping others from loss,
through grief, to recovery.*

- Weekly Grief Tips
- Inspirational Stories
- Articles on Grief
- Resources on Grief
- The Online Source for Grief Help

www.lossgriefandrecovery.com

Order Form

- **Fax Orders:** 904-264-9185
    *Include this order form.

- **Online Orders:** lossgriefandrecovery.com
    *Have your credit card ready.

- **Postal Orders:** Berean Publications, Greg Neal, 4459 US Highway 17 South, Orange Park, Florida, 32003

Title	Quantity	Price	Total
The Journey Through Heartache		$17.95	
An Angel Among Us		$12.00	
Standard Shipping		$4.00	
Sales Tax (Fla. Residents Only)		7%	
Total			

*Express shipping available for an additional charge.

Name: _____

Address: _____

City:_____ State:_____ Zip:_____

Telephone: _____

e-mail address: _____

Payment: ☐ Check ☐ Credit Card
☐ Visa ☐ Master Card ☐ Optima ☐ AMEX ☐ Discover

Card Number: _____

Name on card: _____Exp. date:_____